Instructor's Manual & Test Bank

to accompany

DeVito

Human Communication

Eighth Edition

by

Richard Fiordo
University of North Dakota

 **LONGMAN**

An Imprint of Addison Wesley Longman, Inc.

New York • Reading, Massachusetts • Menlo Park, California • Harlow, England
Don Mills, Ontario • Sydney • Mexico City • Madrid • Amsterdam

Instructor's Manual & Test Bank to accompany DeVito,
Human Communication, Eighth Edition

Copyright © 2000 by Addison Wesley Longman, Inc.

Please visit our website at http://www.awlonline.com

ISBN: 0-321-06308-2

12345678910- -01009900

Table of Contents

Preface

Preface

Contents of the Instructor's Manual

This manual is the *Instructor's Manual and Text Bank for Human Communication: The Basic Course* by Joseph DeVito (8/e). It is designed to assist you in making the basic course in human communication more effective, more interesting and enjoyable, and more rewarding to both you and your students. We also hope it will make your job as an instructor easier.

The *Instructor's Manual* is organized into three distinct sections 1) unit planners, 2) learning by doing, and 3) the test bank. The first section provides for each unit, the goals, discussion or assignment questions, and answers to the applications in the text. This section organizes the text into topical categories for easy term or semester structure. The second section contains several experiential learning activities correlated to each unit. These can be used as exercises for each day in class. Finally, the last section provides true/false and multiple-choice questions for each unit. The three sections are described in detail below:

Unit Planners: Each unit planner contains a pre-planned teaching approach to the individual units in the text which includes the following information:

- *Unit Goals* - The goals of the unit are repeated in this section so that you have a convenient means of focusing on the unit objectives.

- *Instructor Focus* - This section provides approaches to teaching the unit and unique ideas for fun activities in class.

- *Thought Questions* - Thought-provoking question are offered in this section. These questions are designed to stimulate concept application and/or active discussion about the content of the unit. These questions can be used in many ways: class discussions, small group discussions, and writing assignments. Focus answers are also provided.

Learning by Doing: Selected units include a variety of experiential learning activities to practice human communication skills. "Learning by Doing" will help the students to develop practical and effective interpersonal communication skills.

Test Master/Examination Questions and Answers: Over five hundred short-answer questions (true/false and multiple choice) are provided and are keyed to the individual units. This test bank and the individual unit item banks (the list of test questions by units) are computerized for you convenience. To obtain the Test Master disks, contact your Longman sales representative.

Guidelines for the Effective Use of Teaching Human Communication
This collection of teaching aids has been created using personal experiences in teaching human communication in the basic course. We have used these discussion questions and activities, and we know that they are helpful, useful, and effective. We hope that these teaching devices will make your teaching of *Human Communication: The Basic Course* a fulfilling and educational experience. Below you will find hints that we have been effective in the use of these teaching aids.

Thought Questions
- very helpful to start class discussions
- can be used in small groups assigned to different questions followed by brief reports
- can be used for short-answer essay questions
- journal entries can focus on these questions
- use them for reaction papers about various concepts, focusing on applying the concept to the student's experience by explaining or asking what they learned and how the activity relates to real life
- use a "journal" as a course requirement to act as a record of student reactions to the activities in relation to how the concepts apply to them individually

Summary Statement

We encourage you to utilize this *Instructor's Manual*. The manual is process-oriented so that students can gain a better understanding of how to apply the concepts discussed in the text to enhance their communication skills. Applying these communication skills and concepts becomes a way to motivate students to examine human communication. Students explore the concepts discussed in the book to understand their own relationships and examine themselves through the real world in which they all communicate.

This *Instructor's Manual* can make your experiences in teaching human communication as significant as possible. The problem of finding fun, interesting, and suitable material for classwork challenges the Basic Course instructor. Finding a means to develop an understanding of human communication is demanding. The ultimate test of any material, according to author Joseph DeVito, will be in the responses from the students and teachers who use it, in the accomplishments it stimulates, in the insights it encourages, and in the enjoyment it creates. Please feel free to write us; we would love to hear from you. Write to Supplements Department, Longman Publishing, 1185 Avenue of the Americas, New York, NY 10036.

Through the application of the materials in this *Instructor's Manual*, students may come to understand a wide variety of communication forms and the principles governing them. This teaching tool aims to help you apply these communication principles through a variety of teaching approaches. Students will also gain insight into enhancing their personal communication effectiveness.

Richard A. Fiordo
University of North Dakota, 1999.

About the Author

Richard Fiordo (Ph.D., University of Illinois-Urbana) has been teaching Communication for over twenty years. He has taught the basic course in human communication as well as courses in interpersonal communication, small group communication, public speaking and others. Dr. Fiordo is Director of the School of Communication at the University of North Dakota.

Summary Statement

About the Author

Unit Planners

Introduction to the Unit Planners
The Unit Planners in the section contain an organized teaching plan for each of the nineteen units in the text. Each unit planner is divided into three helpful sections:

- *Unit Goals* - an overview of the goals of the unit

- *Instructor Focus* - highlights and hints on how to teach this unit, including unique teaching resources

- *Thought Questions* - thought-provoking questions for interesting discussions and assignments about the concepts in each unit

Each Unit Planner should be utilized as an individualized lesson plan for each area of study in the text. Effective teaching strategies for skill development are included within each unit plan. Suggestions are included for follow-up exercises and activities that may enhance learning in your classroom.

UNIT 1. PRELIMINARIES TO HUMAN COMMUNICATION

Unit Goals. *After completing this unit, you should be able to*

- identify the major types of human communication

- explain the nature of culture and its relevance to human communication

- define <u>communication</u> and its elements: communication context, sources-receivers, encoding-decoding, competence, messages, channel feedback, feedforward, noise, communication effect, and ethics

Instructor Focus. *Helpful hints on what to do in this unit*

1. The author makes the distinction that intercultural communication is involved in all other forms of human communication except intrapersonal. Table 1.1 is extremely important as a summary of not only this unit, but also of the basis for the entire text.

2. The author incorporates self-tests in the text with the first one being in this unit. These are excellent devices for students to test their basic knowledge in various areas. This first one asks students what they believe about communication to test their basic knowledge of that process. As you will note, all the answers are false; the questions illustrate the problems people encounter when they believe in certain communication misconceptions.

3. You will also note that the author has incorporated information and reference to culture in all units. This focus throughout the text allows you as the instructor to integrate cultural references in every unit.

4. Point out to students the author's integration of "learning aid notes" throughout the text. They provide various directions, explanations, or instructions for processing the information.

5. The discussion in this unit on feedback and feedforward are excellent introductory explanations for these concepts.

6. The author also starts his use of Media Watch boxes in this unit. The first one deals with media and ethics by providing some excellent questions about the impact of media on our communication.

Thought Questions. *Thought-provoking questions for interesting discussions and assignments*

1. Explain how communication is a reciprocal process.
    A: The sender and receiver change roles. The answer should be on Table 1.1

3

2. The study of human communication involves the understanding of theory, research, and practical skills for increasing communication effectiveness. Discuss the practical necessity of increasing your own personal communication effectiveness.

     A: Encourage students to investigate the need for better communication strategies with their friends, family, and job.

3. What are some of the types of noise that you experience in your communication? What can you do to stop this noise? Is it always desirable to decrease this noise?

     A: Encourage the student to identify physical and psychological noise they experience and ways of combating these types.

4. What are the seven areas of human communication? Can you distinguish between the seven areas? What makes each unique? Why might it be important to know the differences?

     A: Intrapersonal, interpersonal, small group, organizational, culture, public and mass. Primarily, the type of feedback possible in each area characterizes the area: the first five areas allow for immediate feedback, whereas the last two require delayed feedback. See Table 1.1 for more complete information

UNIT 2: PRINCIPLES OF COMMUNICATION

Unit Goals. After completing this unit, you should be able to

- explain the packaged nature of communication and double-bind messages

- explain interpersonal communication as a transaction

- explain the principle of adjustment in communication

- distinguish between content and relationship dimensions of communication

- define punctuation

- distinguish between symmetrical and complementary transactions

- explain the inevitability and irreversibility of communication

- explain the five major purposes communication serves

Instructor Focus. Helpful hints on what to do in this unit

1. This unit continues to explain the nature of communication by presenting principles essential to understanding communication in all its forms and functions. This is probably best accomplished by illustrating each principle with real life events.

2. Use the author's short dialogued examples to introduce or illustrate the principles. Figure 2.1 provides an excellent visual explanation of the transactional process of communication. Its comparison to linear and interactional processes serve to further illustrate and explain the distinction differences.

Thought Questions. Thought-provoking question for interesting discussions and assignments

1. Explain how communication is a package of signals.
   A: The entire body, verbally and nonverbally, works together to express our thoughts and feelings.

2. Explain how communication is a process of adjustment in close relationships
   A: Since no two persons use identical signal systems, communicators need to take the time to learn and understand the other person's system of signals.

3. What is meant by the term punctuation in communication sequences?
   A: The tendency to divide up various communication transactions in sequences of stimuli and responses for the convenience of processing is known as punctuation. An example of

this would be when each action stimulates the other i.e.--apathetic students when the teacher is not prepared. We begin to ask what behavior was responsible for the other.

4. Give an example of communication as being inevitable.
    A: Students' personal responses about communication being intentional, purposeful and consciously motivated.

5. How are communication components interrelated?
    A: The elements of communication are interdependent, never independent. Each exists in relation to the others.

6. What value is there in understanding another person's signal systems of communication?
    A: Students' personal responses.

7. Why should you think before speaking?
    A: Students should give personal examples of when speaking before thinking had an adverse effect on the communication process within their own relationships.

8. According to the text, what are the five general purposes of communication? Can you create an example of how each one occurs in your life?

    A: To discover (finding out about yourself or learning new information), to establish relationships (relating to friends, family and new acquaintances), to help (assisting someone else through therapy, teaching, parenting), to persuade (motivating behaviors, changing attitudes, and manipulation), and to play (entertainment).

UNIT 3: PERCEPTION

Unit Goals. After completing this unit, you should be able to:

- define <u>perception</u> and explain the three stages in the perception process

- explain how the following processes influence perception: primacy and recency, the self-fulfilling prophecy, perceptual accentuation, implicit personality theory, consistency, stereotyping, and attribution

- explain the strategies for making perceptions more accurate

Instructor Focus. Helpful hints on what to do in this unit

1. An understanding of the influence of perception on meaning is vital. Stress the understanding of this unit because of its value to the rest of the text.

2. Figure 3.1 is very important to the understanding of this unit. Take time to go over this figure with students. Emphasize that the stages of perception overlap occur practically simultaneously.

3. The "Media Watch" box is about cultivation theory or that the media (especially television) are the primary means by which you learn about your society and your culture. Ask students to identify the good and bad aspects of this theory.

4. Have students take the "Self-Test" on perceptual accuracy, which provides general insight into their individual perceptual accuracy, not a specific score. Have students discuss their reactions to the test.

5. In the next section, the author provides for us seven major obstacles to accurate perception of other; with each of these seven types, he also provides the potential obstacles that each is characterized by. This section is hard for students (in my experience) because it is pretty theoretical and the names of the theories are somewhat complex. So, to avoid problems, I suggest you water these down somewhat and to try to think of an example for each that illustrates the theory in more "layperson" terms.

6. Another box in this unit is "Introducing Research." This box gives a rich and simple explanation of the process of research. You can use this to initiate research paper topics and discuss the processes that one goes through to gather data.

7. Don't miss the good advice on making perceptions more accurate.

Thought Questions. *Thought-provoking questions for interesting discussions and assignments*

1. How do you define perception?
   A: The process by which you become aware of the many stimuli impinging on your senses and then accept or reject that stimuli and give it meaning.

2. Describe the three stages of perception and how they relate to each other.
   A: The three states are: sensory stimulation occurs, sensory stimulation is organized, and sensory stimulation is interpreted-evaluated. They occur simultaneously; the states are NOT discrete and separate.

3. The author highlights seven obstacles to making an accurate perception of others. Can you name, identify, and describe each?
   A: The seven are listed under the section called "Processes Influencing Perception."

4. What advice does the author give about reducing uncertainty in perceptions?
   A: The author offers several on page 53.

5. How does the author suggest that you take another's perspective?
   A: The author answers this on page 52 in the box called "Building Communication Skills."

UNIT 4: LISTENING

Unit Goals. *After completing this unit, you should be able to:*

- define listening and explain the five processes involved in listening

- explain the relevance of culture and gender to listening

- define and distinguish between participatory and passive, empathic and objective, nonjudgmental and judgmental, surface and deep, and active and inactive listening

Instructor Focus. *Helpful hints on what to do in this unit*

1. The author provides us with the benefits of effectual listening (see Table 4.1). A great discussion starter is to use these for discussing how listening is different for different people. Students rarely think that thought!

2. The author continues with a "Media Watch" in this unit on page 61, discussing the hot topic of talk radio. This section provides an excellent connection of media and listening--another unique connection.

3. The section on effective listening provides an interesting approach to evaluate your listening effectiveness. A discussion of the five dimensions of listening proves exciting.

Thought Questions. *Thought-provoking questions for interesting discussions and assignments*

1. What are some of the guidelines for regulating participatory and passive listening?
   A: The guidelines include: working at listening, removing distractions, summarizing speaker's thoughts, formulating questions, drawing conclusions between what you hear and already know and assuming that there is value in what the speaker is saying.

2. Explain the statement, "Effective listening includes both nonjudgmental and critical responses."
   A: We need to listen critically with a view toward making a viable judgment or evaluation. When first listening, however, we should keep our mind open in an attempt to listen fairly. Listening with a critical mind will help us to analyze and evaluate a message so that responses can stimulate further examination of ideas.

3. What is the importance of offering feedback to the speaker?
   A: Feedback gives positive confirmation to the speaker, and allows the listener to check his/her interpretation of the speaker's message.

4. Don't we just "pay attention?" Explain the five-state model of listening.
   A: The five stages are all necessary for accurate and effective listening to occur. They are receiving, understanding, remembering, evaluating, and responding. It requires you to participate in the process, not just sit back and "enjoy."

5. Can you identify at least three differences in listening for different cultures?
    A: Answers are listed under the section titled "Listening, Culture, and Gender."

UNIT 5: THE SELF IN COMMUNICATION

Unit Goals. *After completing this unit, you should be able to:*

- define <u>self-concept</u> and explain how it develops

- define <u>self-awareness</u> and explain how it may be increased

- define <u>self-esteem</u> and explain the ways to raise it

- define <u>self-disclosure</u> and explain the factors influencing it and its rewards and dangers

Instructor Focus. *Helpful hints on what to do in this unit*

1. This unit involves four major concepts: self-concept, self-awareness, self-esteem, and self-disclosure. Make sure a clear distinction is made for each of these important variables.

2. Figure 5.1 helps students decide from where the most influence on their self-concept comes. Identifying the sources of the self-concept helps students understand how it is developed and how they can change it. Understanding the way your self-concept develops increases your self-awareness.

3. As you probably remember, students are always fascinated with the Johari Window. Figure 5.2 provides a visual illustration of the concept. Having students draw their perception of their Johari Window is usually very enlightening. Try to provide an example for each quadrant: open, blind, unknown, hidden.

4. Discuss the implications of "outing" in "Media Watch" on page 85.

5. To help students identify their own self-destructive beliefs, have them identify unrealistic drives and discuss how these drives almost always insure failure rather than success.

6. The Self-Test called "How Willing to Self-Disclosure are you?" is an excellent way to have students check their own self-disclosure levels and apprehensions. Also in discussing self-disclosure, discuss the many factors that influence self-disclosure.

7. Discuss the dangers and rewards of self-disclosure. Bring up key concerns related to self-disclosure.

Thought Questions. *Thought-provoking questions for interesting discussions and assignment*

1. Identify and explain the four major areas of the Johari Window.
    A: The four areas include the open self (information, behaviors, attitudes, feelings, desires known to self and others), the blind self (information about ourselves that others know but of which we are ignorant), the unknown self (those parts of ourselves about

11

which neither we nor others know), and the hidden self (contains all you know of yourself and others but keep to yourself).

2. Which areas of the Johari Window have increased your own self-awareness?
    A: Students' personal responses.

3. When is self-disclosure likely to occur?
    A: The potential disclosure can occur when alone with another person or when the discloser feels comfortable with the listener. Other indicators include when the discloser is extroverted or when the disclosure topic is positive.

4. What are the rewards of self-disclosure?
    A: Self-awareness and self-knowledge increases. One can learn to deal more effectively in relationships by increasing his/her communication efficiency.

5. What are the dangers of self-disclosure?
    A: Personal and social rejection form the foundation of the dangers. Intrapersonal difficulties may also arise (i.e. you become ill at ease with telling someone about a personal, private problem).

6. Identify the skills needed when listening to disclosures.
    A: The skills include effective and active listening, supporting and reinforcing the disclosure, keeping the disclosures confidential and not using the disclosures as weapons against the person.

7. What are some of the factors that you have found to have made self-disclosure a rewarding experience?
    A: Students' personal responses could include that communication efficiency and self-knowledge are increased.

8. How has self-disclosure been rewarding to you? What benefits have you received from risking self-disclosure?
    A: Students should provide personal examples of incidences where they were pleased that they took the risk in self-disclosing.

UNIT 6: CULTURE AND COMMUNICATION

Unit Goals. *After completing this unit, you should be able to:*

- define <u>culture</u>, <u>enculturation</u>, and <u>acculturation</u>

- distinguish between collectivist and individualistic orientation, low-and high-context cultures, high and low power distances, and masculine and feminine cultures

- define intercultural communication and explain the general principles for increasing effectiveness in intercultural communication

Instructor Focus. *Helpful hints on what to do in this unit*

1. Start out by asking students what the word culture means to them. You will get some very interesting answers! Then, before doing anything in the unit, have them complete the self-test "What Are Your Cultural Beliefs and Values?" This test provides a value framework from which to work for the remainder of the unit. The explanation after the test is very helpful for you and the students.

2. The author provides four major ways in which cultures differ: collaboration and individualism, low context, power distances, and masculine and feminine. It is important for you to go over these in more simplistic language or you will lose your class. Basically, the differences boil down to 1) whether the culture values the individual or the group, 2) the degree to which information is included in the message or assumed, 3) who has the power, and 4) how the culture views gender.

3. Table 6.1 provides great examples of ethnocentrism. Be sure to go over it with the students to illustrate some of its practical implications.

4. A very important "Media Watch" box deals with cultural imperialism and begins to hit on the topic of cultural superiority, which should make for very interesting discussions. There are some key questions following the illustration.

5. Table 6.2 provides for students a very helpful table of comparisons of people with disabilities. Discuss the "ten commandments" provided.

6. The "Thinking Critically About" section has some excellent summary type questions for this unit. Students could write essays and give short speeches on these topics, or just have a great discussion.

Thought Questions. *Thought-provoking questions for interesting discussions and assignments*

1. Agree or disagree with the statement, "Culture is passed on from one generation to the next through communication, not through genes."
   A: The author supports the statement in the first few pages of the unit.

2. Why is culture NOT synonymous with race or nationality?
    *A: Culture is transferred through communication not through heredity. Culture consists
    of your beliefs, values, ways of communication, and artifacts.*

3. How can an individualistic or collectivist orientation make cultures different? Define those
    terms first and then explain how they apply to the differences in cultures.
    *A: Individualistic cultures promote individual values (power, achievement) and
    collectivist cultures promote collective values (benevolence, tradition, conformity).*

4. What are power distances? How do they affect cultures?
    *A: Cultures can b e categorized by where the power is concentrated (high   power
    distance cultures - Mexico, Brazil, India and low power distance cultures - Denmark,
    Sweden, and the US).*

5. Cultures differ in four major ways. Which do you think is the most relevant or most
    poignant?
    A: Students' individual responses.

6. Do you think the four stages of dealing with culture shock are realistic? Have you
    experienced anything similar to the stages mentioned?
    A: Students' individual responses.

7. The author provides us with principles for improving intercultural communication. First, do
    you think they are realistic? Second, have you used any of them and how?
    A: Students' individual responses.

UNIT 7: VERBAL MESSAGES

Unit Goals. *After completing this unit, you should be able to:*

- identify the characteristics of language and their implications for human communication

- define <u>disconfirmation</u> and <u>confirmation</u> and explain the nature of sexist, hetereosexist, and racist languages as forms of disconfirmation

- explain the suggestions for using verbal messages effectively

Instructor Focus. *Helpful hints on what to do in this unit*

1. The author provides an excellent section on language and meaning. Have students present a skit illustrating each principle of language and meaning described on pages 108-112.

2. The students usually love the section on lying, because nobody thinks they lie, but that others do! Discuss why we really do lie.

3. One of the helpful tests in this unit on page 125-126, is the "Self-Test: When Is Lying Unethical?" Having students complete this exercise will bring up some revealing information for them. Remember, there is no right or wrong answers.

4. The section on gossip is always fascinating to the students. They can't imagine that they would be studying gossip. Have students identify the key components of the use of gossip.

5. The "Media Watch" box deals with cyberspace and electronic communication - a new and fascinating area. Talking about America OnLine and sending e-mail will prove exciting for a class discussion period.

6. There is another "Self-Test: How Confirming Are you?" that will reveal valuable information about the student's confirmation/disconfirmation focus. I maintain that we are generally more disconfirming than we realize, through trying to be funny or using sarcasm. Have students react or write about their test scores.

7. The "Building Communication Skills" box on page 115 has an excellent exercise on confirmation, rejection, and disconfirmation.

8. Another great section in this unit is "How do you lie?" This is something that we all should know. The author provides examples worthy of discussion.

9. Most people do not think or realize how sexist, heterosexist, and racist they may be. This section is revealing. However, the information presented is extremely important (I think it's one of the most important sections of the book). If you can get the students to ask themselves questions and evaluate their communication behaviors regarding these issues, you will have accomplished a great deal.

10. What difference does it make if you use the cultural identifiers as listed in the text? Can't we all just be people and not worry about how we are identified by others? What's the issue here?

11. Why is sexist language so offensive to some people?

12. Why do we confuse fact and inference? Can't we tell the difference?

13. Explain the statement "Meanings are in people, not in words." How does this statement relate to bypassing?

14. To demonstrate how to use verbal messages effectively (see page 119), divide the class into seven groups and assign a "conceptual distortion" to each group. Have them develop a skit to illustrate their characteristics. Have them also provide the solutions for correcting the problems caused by the use of the conceptual distortion. All this information is provided in the text.

15. The "Self-Test" called "Can you Distinguish the Facts from Inference?" (see page 121), is an excellent way to have students check their ability to distinguish between fact and inference. Many people do not distinguish very well between these two. This test helps point that out.

Thought Questions. *Thought-provoking questions for interesting discussions and assignments*

1. Explain the statement "meanings are in people, not in words."
   A: Answers should focus on individual frame of reference, individual perception, symbolism of words, the arbitrariness of those symbols, and how words can mean so many different things (i.e. have students draw or bring in a picture of what they see as beautiful).

2. How can meaning be influenced by the context in which it is sent?
   A: The context (situation, location, reason for being there, etc.) greatly impact upon how and why the meaning of a message is interpreted.

3. Can a word be both denotative and connotative? What do these terms mean? Do you use more denotative language or connotative language?
   A: Yes, words can be both, but are primarily used to express one or the other. Denotative is an objective definition and connotative is the subjective feeling. When students examine their language, they will detect many hidden meanings in their word choice.

4. What are indirect messages? Why do people use them? Why don't people say what they really mean? Do you think you say what you really mean?
   A: Honest feelings are difficult to express in words alone. Indirect messages allow us to express a desire without offending anyone. They allow us to observe the rules of polite interaction. We feel that it is difficult to be honest because then others know how we

feel and then they can use this information against us. If we are honest, we have to be responsible - and that's hard for some people.

5. Why is honesty such a big issue in relationships? Is it possible to be totally honest in a relationship (according to the definition given in the text)? Is it even desirable to be totally honest in a relationship?
    A: While everyone usually claims that honesty is the most important value or virtue in a relationship, it is also the least followed or adhered to by many. Most people think they are really honest, but when it comes right down to it, we all lie. What we do is justify the lie by making excuses, etc.

6. Which reason for lying do you think people use the most?
    A: Students' individual responses.

7. What is gossip? Why do people gossip? Is it bad to gossip?
    A: Gossip is defined as idle talk or rumor, especially about the personal or private affairs of others. It is a frequent, prevalent, and enjoyable form of communication. Gossip is bad when it is unethical or breaks a bond of confidentiality.

8. What are some of the ways in which you can create a confirming communication climate?
    A: See the Self-Test on pages 112-113.

9. Do you think you use racist, sexist or heterosexist language? Can you provide an example of each of these types of disconfirmation?
    A: Students' individual responses.

UNIT 8: NONVERBAL MESSAGES

Unit Goals. After completing this unit, you should be able to

- define nonverbal communication and identify its major functions

- define the nonverbal channels and provide examples of the messages that can be communicated through each

- explain how nonverbal messages are influenced by culture

Instructor Focus. Helpful hints on what to focus on in this unit

1. Students always enjoy the optic of nonverbal communication. The ways in which non verbal messages are used with verbal messages are very important. Be sure to provide an example of each or have students come up with examples.

2. The "Relationships and Professional Distances" box in Table 8.1 offers four different distances. Discuss how we use space during the normal course of communicating.

3. This unit covers a great deal of the nonverbal codes: body, face, eyes, vocal sounds, silence, and time. While the material is not overwhelming, it is cumbersome, so tread lightly. Students are usually fascinated by this unit because the concepts seem very real to them. Help them relate what they learn to their own personal lives.

4. Be sure students understand the five types of body movement: emblem, illustrators, affect displays, regulators, and adaptors. The best way to do this is to have them demonstrated. Select people from the class that can and will demonstrate one of the five. Then have the class discuss its function in the communication process.

5. The four facial management techniques are things the students use all the time without realizing it. Again, have these demonstrated by class members. You can even make up a little scene to go along with the technique. The "Understanding Theory and Research" box on page 133 will help you.

6. Have students address the statement, "The eyes are regarded as the most important nonverbal message system."

7. Rarely do we think of the functions of eye contact except to see; but there are specific functions the author provides that are very important. Be sure to point these out.

8. The sound of the voice is a very powerful nonverbal message. We can completely change the meaning of a message through the use of the voice. Have students demonstrate this with A-B-C language in a skit which you create the focus. See if the class can identify the emotion or general meaning just from the tone of voice. There are also two items in the "Thinking Critically About" section which deal with linguistics.

9. Silence is not often studied or even thought of as an area to study. However, silence communicates LOUDLY. Be sure to go over the functions of silence as presented by the author. They are very important to the understanding of the impact of silence.

10. Most people have no idea that their use of time sends nonverbal messages. The section on chronemics has excellent coverage on the major components as related to this topic. The definitions are easy and students quickly get into the discussion. One idea that I use is for students to take off their watches for the class period; then talk about how that feels. You might be surprised.

11. This unit covers different nonverbal codes: proxemics, territoriality, touch, smell and artifactual communication. My experience is that students love to talk about nonverbal communication. It fascinates them. Demonstrations seem to work best with this material.

12. Table 8.1 illustrates the four proxemic distances people use daily. Have these visually demonstrated in class.

13. Another way to illustrate the influences on space communication to assign the factors to groups and have them present a little skit. The influences include: culture, status, context, subject matter, sex, age.

14. The theories about space are quite interesting. Again, demonstrate the theories visually.

15. Territoriality is one of my favorite codes. It demonstrates how possessive Americans are. Your author identifies two dimensions of territoriality: territorial types and markers. Have groups of students demonstrate each.

16. One of the things students love to do is to take a picture of a human body and then shade in the areas in which someone is allowed to touch (mother, father, best friend, close intimate friend, teacher). They soon realize how many rules they have, and they also learn something about boundaries.

17. The "Self-Test" on page 141 called "Do You Avoid Touch?" is an excellent test to evaluate student touch avoidance behaviors. As indicated, the higher the score, the higher the touch avoidance.

18. How can color be a nonverbal communication message?

19. The "Media Watch" box on "Legible Clothing" on page 139 is great. It talks about how advertisers have convinced us to wear clothes with their labels on them, which end up being advertisements for the designer. Discuss the statement, "Legible clothing communicates lower status and lack of power."

20. Do you think people judge you by the clothing you wear? Why or why not?

Thought Questions. *Thought-provoking questions for interesting discussions and assignments*

1. Identify and explain the five classes of nonverbal movement. Give examples of each movement.
    A: Emblems directly substitute translated words or phrases (thumb sign for hitchhiking); illustrators accompany verbal messages (hands far apart when speaking of something large); affect displays communicate emotional meaning (smile for happiness); regulators monitor or control the speaking of another (hand gesture to indicate slowing down); and adaptors help satisfy a personal need (scratching one's head).

2. What are some functions of eye movements?
    A: Eye movements may serve to seek feedback, to inform others to speak, to signal the nature of a relationship, and to compensate for increased physical distance.

3. What does the pupil size indicate in terms of nonverbal communication?
    A: Pupil size seems to be indicative of one's interest, and one's level of emotional arousal. Pupils enlarge when one is interested in something, or when one is emotionally aroused in a positive way.

4. What are some of the eye avoidance functions?
    A: Eye avoidance can signal lack of interest. It can also block out unpleasant stimuli or close off visual stimuli, thus heightening the other senses.

5. How can we signal power through visual dominance behavior?
    A: The average speaker maintains a high level of eye contact while listening and a lower level while speaking. When powerful individuals want to signal dominance, they may reverse the pattern.

6. What personal adaptors are acceptable in public? Which ones are NOT acceptable?
    A: While the response to this question can be very broad, some suggested acceptable adaptors might include scratching your nose, pulling your hair away from your face, fixing your clothing, and wetting your lips. Unacceptable adaptors might include scratching your groin, picking your nose, and scratching your butt.

7. What are some of the rules we have in our society about eye contact?
    A: Some rules might include where (part of the body), how and how long you look at someone. For example, length of gaze is restricted in our society because it indicates interest, usually sexual. When men stare at a woman's breasts, that gaze's location is considered rude.

8. In what instances, personal or professional, was eye contact a crucial factor in establishing a positive relationship?
    A: Students might focus on initial encounters with others as well as their own personal experiences.

9. Do regulators enhance the flow of communication? Is it more difficult to establish a smooth flow of communication over the phone when regulators are not pronounced?
    A: Students' personal responses.

10. Identify and explain the four proxemic distances.
    A: The four major distances include: intimate distance, ranging from actual touching to 18 inches; personal distance, ranging from 1 1/2 feet to 4 feet; social distance, ranging from 4 to 12 feet; and public distance, ranging from 12 to 25 feet.

11. What factors influence treatment of space?
    A: Status, culture, context, subject matter, sex, age and positive or negative evaluation of the other person all influence the treatment of space.

12. Identify and explain the term territoriality.
    A: Territoriality refers to one's possessive reaction to an area of space or to particular objects. Territoriality can be innate according to some researchers, or it may be a learned behavior that is culturally based.

13. Identify several meanings and functions of touch.
    A: Touch may communicate positive emotions; our intention to play. Touch may also direct the behaviors, attitudes, and feelings of the other person as such control may communicate a number of messages. Touch may be ritualistic and centers on greetings and departures. Task-related touching is associated with the performance of some function.

14. What are some of the reasons that we tend to avoid touch?
    A: Touch avoidance, which refers to our desire to avoid touching and being touched by others, has been found to be related to communication apprehension, self-disclosure, age, and sex.

15. If someone treats space differently than you do (i.e. a sales person moves from a social space to a personal distance), what is your first reaction? Does this encroachment affect the communication taking place? How?
    A: Students' personal responses.

16. When has your instinct to touch had a positive effect? A negative one?
    A: Students' personal responses.

17. How does smell qualify as a nonverbal message
    A: Students' personal responses.

18. Give an example of an artifact that you use/wear/etc. and tell what it communicates and why you use it.
    A: Students' personal responses.

UNIT 9: INTERPERSONAL COMMUNICATION: CONVERSATION

Unit Goals. *After completing this unit, you should be able to:*

- explain the five-step model of conversation

- explain the processes and skills involved in managing conversations

- explain the nature and functions of the disclaimer and the excuse

Instructor Focus. *Helpful hints on what to focus on in this unit*

1. Have the students take the "Self-Test" on pages 160-162 called "How Flexible Are You in Communication?" This test gives students a general view of conversation. Discussion will bring up some key values, upon which the test hits. The last question in this section is an excellent one, and could even be used as a writing or speaking assignment.

2. Figure 9.1 provides readers with a view of the process of conversation. While the steps or stages are simple, make sure the students know how to distinguish between them.

3. There is quite a large section devoted to maintaining conversations which focus on turn-taking. This is not a topic we talk about often. Those five "turn-taking" cues say a great deal abut how you operate within a relationship. It's always so rewarding to see students turn on the light bulb suddenly.

4. There is a great group of situations listed on page 161 in a "Building Communication Skills" box on "How do You Close a Conversation?" These four situations provide an excellent way of checking up on the students understanding of the concepts.

5. The "Self-Test" called "Are You a High Self-Monitor?" on pages 166-167 is highly useful. Take the test and find out!

6. The "Media Watch" section on page 168 discusses "the spiral of silence." Have your students apply this theory to their everyday lives.

Thought Questions. *Thought-provoking questions for interesting discussions and assignments*

1. Have students discuss Figure 9.1 on page 153, "The Process of Conversation," by asking "how accurately do you think this model reflects the normal progression of a conversation?"

2. Do the "what's your line?" exercise on opening conversations in the section on "Understanding Theory and Research" by having students role play the basic types of opening lines. It clearly demonstrates the difficulty people have in starting conversations. Discuss why.

3. The section on turn-taking cues is a fascinating one. Speakers and listeners can both use these techniques to manipulate the conversation, or at least influence its direction. Have students role play the situations provided in the text or make up their own. Figure 9.2 on page 159 provides an excellent visual chart for those cues.

4. Debate the following statement: "Effectiveness or competence in conversation and following the appropriate conversational rules will contribute to your own interpersonal attractiveness."

5. On pages 160-162, the "Self-Test" on "How Flexible Are You in Communication?" is extremely valuable in helping you decide if you are flexible in your communication. This is a hard trait to crack because most people think they ARE flexible. The test is a good one and should raise some pretty poignant questions for discussion.

6. The "Self-Test" on page 166-167 is "Are You a High Self-Monitor?" It measures your level of self-monitoring in public. Discuss these questions: "In what situations and with what people are you most likely to self-monitor? Least likely to self-monitor? How do these situations and people differ?"

7. On page 170 under "Preventing Conversational Problems: The Disclaimer," the author provides us with five types of disclaimers used to prevent problems. Which ones do you use? Why? What are the results of its use for you?

8. The section on excuses on page 170 is great. Don't we all play that game? This section puts it in black and white for us to understand. Ask students to identify kinds of excuses they use and watch the fur fly!

UNIT 10: INTERPERSONAL RELATIONSHIPS

Unit Goals. After completing this unit, you should be able to:

- explain the factors and processes involved in interpersonal relationship development, deterioration, maintenance, and repair

- explain the types of friendships, loves, and primary relationships that have been identified

- explain the basic assumptions of attraction, relationship rules, reinforcement, social exchange, and equity theories

Instructor Focus. Helpful hints on what to focus on in this unit

1. What are the three dynamic tensions between the polar opposites within relationships? Identify each and describe how they function.

2. The author emphasizes the six stages of relationships with his model in figure 10.1. He stresses how all relationships are different and can not necessarily fit into a model. He feels that at best, the model provides a way to talk about relationships.

3. On page 191, the "Media Watch" section on parasocial relationships is an interesting phenomena. Students will be fascinated to discuss this issue and usually have lots of examples from parents and grandparents who demonstrate these characteristics.

4. The author provides five different relationship theories, each distinct in its own way. Have students divide up and assign one of the theories to each of five groups. Have each group prepare a short skit depicting the characteristics of their assigned theory.

5. The section on page 199 on "Thinking Critically About" query the five theories in some way. Use these questions for class discussions.

6. Remind students that the research referred to in this text is based on research conducted in the United States. This means that it reflects our cultural biases, so the statements made refer ONLY to people from the U.S.

7. Have students brainstorm for reasons for relationship development. Why do they form relationships in the first place?

8. In the "Media Watch" section on page 191, the focus is on parasocial relationships. Go over the illustrations presented.

9. The "Self-Test" on page 189 called "What Type of Relationship Do You Prefer?" provides students with a measure of the relationships they choose. Discuss the reasons the students offer.

10. It is fun for students to analyze their current relationships. Have them select one relationship which has been terminated by one party or the other. While the text provides reasons, students can develop their own as well.

11. The next section talks about relationship maintenance. Discuss the reasons students stay in relationships. Again student can create their own.

12. The author provides several lists of maintenance behaviors. Have students identify one in particular that they use (or have used) and describe its use.

13. Something that warrants some discussion is the self-repair issue. We are never taught these kinds of skills, which are vitally necessary for survival.

14. This unit talks about special relationships and love. It really hits home for the students. This unit will help provide more success to students in love relationships.

15. Consider the list of traits particular to friendship relationships on page 187.

16. One fun thing to do (and students seem to like it, too) is to create a list of essential characteristics for any friendship. The author provides us with several, but what would the classes' list look like?

17. One of the things that students get excited about are the types of love. The author's coverage of this information is excellent and begins on page 187.

18. The "Self-Test" called "What Kind of Lover Are You?" on page 187 is excellent. Students like to discover their scores for this self-test.

19. An important discussion is the topic of primary relationships. Most students still think only of the traditional family. Ask students to voice their opinions abut different types of primary relationships.

20. It is important for students to be familiar with the communication patterns in primary relationships and families as explained by the author. The patterns may very well help some students to characterize their relationships in ways they had not thought of previously.

Thought Questions. *Thought-provoking questions for interesting disucssions and assignments*

1. What are the six relationship stages (refer to figure 10.1)?
    A: The six stages include: contact, involvement, intimacy, deterioration, repair, and dissolution.

2. Identify how relationships vary in breadth and depth.
    A: The number of topics about which you communicate is referred to as breadth. The degree to which the inner personality is penetrated is referred to as depth.

3. Explain what is meant by the term "matching hypothesis."
   A: The "match hypothesis" holds that we mate and date those who are about equivalent to ourselves in physical attractiveness.

4. As a written assignment, select a relationship you've had that has ended. Write a 2-3 page analysis of that relationship correlating it to the six stages in the text.
   A: Students' personal responses.

5. Of the five theories presented, which theory of relationships do you follow for the most part? Can you give an example? Do you think they overlap?
   A: Students' personal responses.

6. What are some of the reasons that relationships develop?
   A: Students may answer according to their own experiences. Answers should include: to lessen loneliness, to secure stimulation, to acquire self-knowledge, and to maximize pleasures and minimize pains.

7. The "Self-Test" called "How Apprehensive Are You in Conversations?" provides students with a measure of apprehension in normal conversations. List two test items.
   A: 1) I have no fear of speaking in conversations and 2) I'm afraid to speak up in conversations.

8. What are the major phrases involved in initiating relationships?
   A: Three may be identified in initiating relationships: examining the qualifiers, determining clearance, and communicating your desire for contact.

9. Identify and explain the nonverbal behaviors which are useful in the first encounter.
   A: The following nonverbal behaviors are useful in the first encounter: establish eye contact, signal positive response, concentrate your focus, establish proximity, maintain an open posture, and reinforce positive behaviors.

10. Identify and explain the verbal behaviors which are useful in the first encounter.
    A: The following verbal behaviors are helpful in the first encounter: introduce yourself, focus the conversation on the other person, exchange favors and rewards, be energetic, stress the positives, avoid negative or too intimate self-disclosures, and establish commonalities.

11. What are some of the causes for relationship deterioration?
    A: Among the causes for relationship deterioration are: the diminishing of the reasons for establishing the relationship, relational changes, unrealistic expectations, sexual dissatisfaction, work-related problems, and financial difficulties.

12. What nonverbal and verbal behaviors should you (or do you) employ when you first become interested in someone? What behaviors receive the most favorable reaction?
    A: Students' personal responses.

13. After studying the steps in initiating relationships and the causes for deterioration, what measures can be taken to keep a relationship healthy? In what instances is breaking up the best alternative?

    A: Students' personal responses.

14. How does your list of friendship types compare with those your author presents? Were any of yours the same or similar?

    A: Students' personal responses.

15. If you disagree with the author's types of friendship as presented on page 187, how would you describe them differently?

    A: Students' personal responses.

16. Which type of love do you think you are involved in the most? Explain.

    A: Students' personal responses.

17. The "Self-Test" called "What kind of lover are you?" is fun. What does it tell you about yourself? Did you learn anything you didn't like?

    A: Students' personal responses.

18. How do you communicate love to someone? Can you make a list of behaviors?

    A: Students' personal responses.

19. Are you a traditionalist, an independent, or a separate? How does that affect your relationships, especially with your family?

    A: Students' personal responses.

20. Which of the five relationship theories have you used? Why? How?

    A: Students' personal responses.

21. What guidance can you gather from the author for communication in friendship, love and primary relationships?

    A: Students' personal responses.

UNIT 11: INTERPERSONAL CONFLICT

Unit Goals. *After completing this unit, you should be able to:*

- define interpersonal conflict and distinguish between content and relationship conflict

- explain the strategies of conflict and distinguish between content and relationship conflict

- explain the strategies of conflict management

- describe the suggestions for preparing for and following up an interpersonal conflict

Instructor Focus. *Helful hints on what to focus on in this unit*

1. This unit covers the nature of conflict and conflict management. The unit describes unproductive conflict management strategies. Going over these will be most helpful.

2. Spend some time considering what myths about conflict students buy into. Then seek to dispel them. For example, the major myth about conflict is that it is bad and dangerous. Discuss with your students how conflict makes us think; that is, how conflict can be good and helpful.

3. It is VERY important to distinguish between content and conflict and relationship conflict. They are both two separately distinctive items for consideration. Table 11.1 on page 202 is especially helpful here.

4. Another important distinction about conflict is to identify its context: physical, sociopsychological, temporal, and cultural. Ask students to identify the context of their conflict examples.

5. Have students make a list of the positives and negatives they see about conflict. Then initiate a discussion about these lists. This should help them identify that conflict has both.

6. Be sure to spend adequate time on page 205 on the "Understanding Theory and Research" box on "Do women and men fight the same way?" It provides an in-depth look at that process and provides a very solid foundation for examining the differences.

7. A large portion of the chapter is spent on unproductive conflict management strategies. Take time to go over each and illustrate how they work and function in a conflict situation. Students will recognize these strategies and will now know what to call them. The "Building Communication Skills" box on "How Do We Find win-win Solutions?" on page 208, will be helpful. See also the two "Self-Test" sections in verbal aggressiveness and argumentativeness on pages 212-214.

Thought Questions. *Thought-provoking questions for interesting discussions and assignments*

1. Of the several unproductive conflict management methods, which one do you think is the most dangerous or harmful in relationships?

2. What do you think the myths about conflict are? Which ones do you/did you believe in? Did you change your mind? Why or why not.

3. What's the difference between the content and relationship aspects of conflict? Why is it important to distinguish between these two categories? Which one is more powerful? Can you provide an example that illustrates these concepts?

4. Highlight the context of an example of conflict by identifying the physical, sociopsychological, temporal or cultural dimensions of it.

5. Do you agree that conflict has both negative and positive aspects? Explain your answer.

6. Identify the specific conflict management strategies that you use and provide an example for each. If you use ALL of them, limit your examples to four.

7. Take the two self-tests on pages 212 and 213 which measure your verbal aggressiveness and argumentativeness. Discuss the results in class.

8. What advice does the author give about what to do before and after a conflict.

UNIT 12: INTERVIEWING

Unit Goals. *After completing this unit, you should be able to:*

- define <u>interviewing</u> and its major types

- describe the sequence of steps for information interviews

- explain the principles of employment interviewing

- distinguish between lawful and unlawful questions

Instructor Focus. *Helpful hints on what to focus on in this unit*

1. This unit describes various formats and types of interviews in which students could be involved. An important concept described in this unit is the informational interview. Seniors can use one or more of these just to expose themselves to the job market. When students say they are doing it for a class requirement, companies are eager to help.

2. The "Media Watch" section on page 222 highlights an important aspect of media, namely talk shows, a form of interview. The article asks some poignant questions and hits some very key issues. Use it as a discussion starter.

3. Much practical advice is given in this unit, especially about information interviews. Especially look at pages 224-225.

4. The "Understanding Theory and Research" box on page 226 gives an indication of why some people fail at interviews. It is extremely important for students to be aware of being talkaholics, so that they do not fall into this trap.

5. There are some excellent hints for resumes on page 228. Make sure students are aware of these points. You might want to have them create a resume as an assignment, using page 228 as a guide.

6. The "Self-Test" on page 229 provides students with an excellent measure of their apprehension on employment interviews. The test is simple and the scoring easy. Ask students to comment on the results.

7. Table 12.1 on page 231 provides students with a list of potential questions they should practice answering. You could go around the room and have students answer one of these questions. It's great practice.

8. Students always get excited when you talk about unlawful questions. This unit does an excellent job highlighting the problem areas here. The "Self-Test" on page 233 provides a sample test.

Thought Questions. *Thought-provoking questions for interesting discussions and assignments*

1. What types of interviews have you been on in the past? Which one was the most difficult? Why?
   A: Students' individual responses.

2. How do interviews differ from interpersonal communication?
   A: Interviews differ in format and purpose; the format is usually through question and answer, while the purpose has specific goals.

3. Let's brainstorm for all the things you need to do to prepare for an interview. Where would you start?
   A: While the book gives several suggestions, this list could be endless. Just focus on important preparation of question, answers, nonverbals (clothing, facial expression, mannerisms), and resume.

4. Let's make a list of "dos and don'ts" for communication behaviors during an interview.
   A: Some dos: smile, use direct eye contact, sit up straight, keep feet flat, be friendly, be conservative. Some don'ts: no gum, no playing with hands, don't be late, no fidgeting.

5. What's the most important follow-through procedure after the interview?
   A: To send a typed thank you note would probably be the highest preference, but also important would be to analyze your strengths and weaknesses demonstrated in the interview for future improvement.

6. (Female student's name), how would you answer this unlawful question in an employment interview? "So, do you plan on having children soon?" (Male student's name), how would you answer this unlawful question in an employment interview? "What language do you speak at home?"
   A: Students' individual responses. As text explains, interviewees have a choice in answering. If you do not want to provide the information sought through an unlawful question, be gentle at first, then courteous but firm, and finally very direct.

UNIT 13: SMALL GROUP COMMUNICATION

Unit Goals. *After completing this unit, you should be able to*

- describe the nature of a small group, its stages and formats

- explain the four principles of brainstorming

- describe the types of nature of personal growth groups

- explain the function of the learning groups and focus group

- identify the steps that should be followed in problem-solving discussions

Instructor Focus. *Helpful hints on what to focus on in this unit*

1. This unit has some unfamiliar terms. So to help out, water them down or use familiar words for descriptions.

2. Review the author's definition of a small group. Use the author's definition on page 239.

3. Have students do the "Self-Test" on page 239 called "How apprehensive are you in group discussions?"

4. An important section is "Power in the Small Group" starting on page 244. These categories by French and Raven are universal and apply to all types of power in most contexts. Have students figure out which type they use when they are the leader.

5. Brainstorming is another important term in this unit that deserves attention. It is a technique that students will probably use in their day-to-day lives. Explain the steps clearly because most people misuse this technique. See page 248.

6. Figure 13.2 on page 248 provides for us the four major small group formats in a very visual method. Have students explain each.

7. The "Building Communication Skills" box on page 257 contains valuable advice on how to listen to new ideas. The author's derivation of PIP'N provides a valuable tool for your listening repertoire. Students like this technique.

8. Students may be challenged by the different types of groups covered in this unit. It might be helpful if you categorized the types on the blackboard for them.

9. Dewey's famous problem-solving sequence is visually depicted for the students in Figure 13.3 on page 253. This chart makes its procedures very clear.

10. The "Understanding Theory and Research" box on page 255 identifies methods of evaluation for research. It provides the question to ask to make sure your research is accurate and valid. Look especially at the differences between results and conclusions.

Thought Questions. *Thought-provoking questions for interesting discussions and assignments*

1. How can small group communication be characterized?
    A: The key features revolve around the similarity of the members, the commonality of goals and the organizational structure used to communicate.

2. Can you name some of the norms used by a group to which you belong?
    A: Students' individual responses. Issues around time, schedules, procedures, dress, duties, and dues are primary.

3. How can a group member discover the norms of a group?
    A: Some norms are written down (explicit) as specific policies or procedures (i.e. meetings start at 7 p.m. sharp), while other norms are assumed (implicit) (i.e. proper dress is essential for acceptance). The implicit norms can only be learned through observation of nonverbal cues.

4. Select a type of group to which you currently belong or have belonged. Briefly describe in a one-page typed paper how this group fit one of the types listed in the text.
    A: Students' individual assignments; discussion could follow relating specific examples of various types of groups.

5. What are the rules for brainstorming? Why are these rules necessary for effective brainstorming to occur?
    A: There are four general rules:
    1. Don't criticize.
    2. Strive for quantity.
    3. Combine and extend ideas.
    4. Develop the wildest ideas possible.
    Primarily, for brainstorming to work, participants have to feel completely free to contribute without judgment or evaluation. This promotes free thinking and creativity.

6. Of the small group formats, which is most appropriate for a student council to solve a tuition increase debate?
    A: The panel or round table lends itself most appropriately.

7. What is the difference between a colloquy and a symposium? How might each be used most effectively?
    A: A colloquy uses experts sharing in a panel or round table discussion with a moderator who fields questions from the audience; a symposium uses prepared speeches by panelists with a leader and no audience interaction. A colloquy is effective for controversial topics, while a symposium seeks the expertise of sharing knowledge and points of view from experts.

8. Dewey's problem-solving approach utilizes six steps designed to make solutions more efficient and effective. Let's select a problem as a class and go through the six steps to see how they work in application. What is an important issue to students currently? (After the issue is selected, go through the following steps together as a class.) The six steps are:

- define and analyze the problem
- establish criteria for evaluating solutions
- identify possible solutions
- evaluate solutions
- select the best solution(s)
- test selected solution(s)

UNIT 14: MEMBERS AND LEADERS

Unit Goals. *After completing this unit, you should be able to*

- identify the three major types of member roles and give examples of each type

- explain the theories of leadership, the three leadership styles, and the functions leaders serve in small group communication

- explain the influence of culture on group membership and leadership

Instructor Focus. *Helpful hints on what to focus on in this unit*

1. An important part of this unit is the list of task roles, maintenance roles, and individual roles. Everyone can identify with these roles that are played in all groups. Have students identify which ones they play.

2. This chapter covers the concept of groupthink on page 264. It is important and should not be missed. There is an excellent movie called "Groupthink" which you might want to consider showing. It points out the dangers of everyone thinking alike.

3. Table 14.2 on page 266 summarizes the four approaches to leadership. However, the styles of leadership section on page 269 is important to the overall scheme of things also. Review both.

4. The "Self-Test" on pages 267-268 is enlightening for students to discover what kind of leader they might be. Many are surprised at the results.

5. The author discusses major functions of leadership. He also notes that these functions are not the exclusive property of the leaders; however, when there is a specific leader, he/she is expected to perform them. Students are usually surprised at some of these. Review them.

6. The "Understanding Theory and Research" box on page 271 reveals the qualities of the effective leader and is always good for a class discussion. Ask the author's question of your class: "What can you learn from Attila the Hun?"

7. An important concept to go over is the one discussed in "Media Watch" on page 273. The concept of agenda-setting theory is quite important, especially if we are unaware of it.

Thought Questions. *Thought-provoking questions for interesting discussions and assignments*

1. As a group member, what is your main job?
   A: Although this appears to be a "trick" question, the point to is start a discussion on giving up individual needs for the group's needs - something not done very often by group members.

2. Which group task roles do you think you play in groups? Which group building and maintenance roles do you think you play in groups? Which individual roles do you think you play in groups?

    A: Students' individual responses. Students should be able to identify one or two roles they play in each dimension; however, some students may be more task-oriented. The key here is to have them identify roles they see themselves playing.

3. Do you think you have ever been a victim of "groupthink?" Can you describe the situation?

    A: Students' individual responses.

4. Why does the situational leadership style make sense? Or does it?

    A: Situational leadership takes into consideration the needs of the group at the moment and focuses on helping the group meet those needs.

5. Can anyone describe a group in which you have served that had a laissez-faire leader? How about a democratic leader? An authoritarian leader? Was the leadership style used effective or ineffective? Why?

    A: Students' individual responses. Here the instructor will want to stress the different types of leadership that work in some situations and do not work in others. None of the three major styles have negative connotations except when inappropriate to the group's needs.

6. Describe the functions carried out by an effective group leader.

    A: The book provides these major ones:
    - *activate group interaction*
    - *maintain effective interaction*
    - *keep members on track*
    - *ensure member satisfaction*
    - *encourage ongoing evaluation and improvement*
    In addition, refer to pages 270-274

7. What do you think the leader's major functions are?

    A: Guide the students here to break from their myths about leadership and identify the variety of styles possible and appropriate.

8. What are some of the problems you see that limit the effectiveness of the group? Let me start off with on - personal goals taking precedence over group goals. What things have you experienced in groups that you have noticed reduce their effectiveness as a group?

    A: While there can be a multitude of answers here, the text focuses on several key points.

UNIT 15: TOPIC, AUDIENCE, AND RESEARCH

Unit Goals. After completing this unit, you should be able to:

- define public speaking and explain the methods for managing communication apprehension

- explain the nature of suitable public speaking topics and purposes and how to select and narrow them

- explain the factors that need to be considered in audience analysis

- explain the strategies and sources for researching speech topics

Instructor Focus. Helpful hints on what to focus on in this unit

1. The second section is about apprehension in public communication. It names what it is, when it occurs, and how one copes with it. This is one of the best sections I have ever read about apprehensive communication. It warrants some articulation.

2. The "Self-Test" on page 282 measures how apprehensive you are in public speaking situations. Ask students if it is valid for them.

3. One part is about audience analysis. I think, for this course, it is challenging and thorough. Pages 289-294 will be of help here.

Thought Questions. Thought-provoking questions for interesting discussions and assignments

1. What is your biggest fear when experiencing apprehension in public communication? What are some of the ways of dealing with it?

2. How many - honestly - have some fear about giving a speech in front of an audience. How many scored above 18 on the public speaking section on the "How Apprehensive Are you?" test in the text? A score above 18 indicates some degree of apprehension; however, there are some things you can do to deal with speaker apprehension. Can anyone name them?
   A: You can prepare and practice thoroughly, gain experiences, put apprehension in perspective and use physical activity and deep breathing to help relax the body.

3. How many have given a speech before this class? What are some hints you can offer to the class on how to be an effective speaker?
   A: Students' individual responses. Instructor may want to offer a few ideas: be yourself by speaking conversationally, look directly at your audience to make them your friends, practice a lot, smile and take a deep breath before you start, and choose a topic you are really interested in.

4. What are the topoi? What do they have to do with topics? See the author's practical account on page 287.

5. The section on audience willingness on page 292 is valuable. When you haven't got willingness, you haven't got much. Discuss this.

6. The "Building Communication Skills" box on page 302 shares some important concerns about electronic research. Have you ever conducted research through a computer search? How did you proceed and with what results?

UNIT 16: SUPPORTING AND ORGANIZING YOUR SPEECH

Unit Goals. After completing this unit, you should be able to:

- explain how a thesis may be developed and how major propositions may be derived from it

- explain how propositions may be supported with a wide variety of appropriate materials such as examples, testimony, statistics, and presentation aids

- explain the major patterns for organizing a public speech

- explain the functions and methods for introducing and concluding the speech for connecting its parts

Instructor Focus. Helpful hints on what to focus on in this unit

1. The unit explains presentation aids and media at length. This begins on page 314. Presentation media and aids assist all students. Discuss strategies with your class for using diverse presentation aids and media.

2. This unit provides a long list of organizational patterns for public speaking. Have groups of student select and demonstrate each of those listed. You might want to help them distinguish these patterns: problem-solution, cause-effect, effect-cause, structure-function, and claim-and-proof.

3. The motivated sequence organizational pattern deserves special attention. Have students explain each of its five steps. You might assist them in relating one part to another. Commercials are useful in showing the motivated sequence in action, and there is no current shortage of commercials.

Thought Questions. Thought-provoking questions for interesting discussions and assignments

1. What additional forms of support does your author provide?
   A: See Table 16.1 on page 310.

2. Do the ends justify the means?
   A: Base answers on "Understanding Theory and Research" on page 312.

3. What typefaces are best to choose? Please consider how easy each is to read and how consistent in tone each is to your speech.
   A: Base answers on Table 16.2 on page 324.

4. What are the steps in the motivated sequence? Explain each.
   A: Attention, need, satisfaction, visualization and action. Details can be found on page 326.

5. Illustrate problem-solution and effect-cause patterns of organizations. Explain differences.
   A: Students' individual responses.

UNIT 17: STYLE AND DELIVERY IN PUBLIC SPEAKING

Unit Goals. *After completing this unit, you should be able to*

- explain the values of outlining and the structure and function of the preparation, skeletal, and delivery outlines

- explain how to achieve an oral style that is clear, vivid, appropriate, personal, and forceful

- explain the suggestions for efficient and effective rehearsal and the advantages and disadvantages of the different methods of delivery and the characteristics of effective vocal and bodily delivery

Instructor Focus. *Helpful hints on what to focus on in this unit*

1. This unit addresses the concepts of public communication: speaker, listener, noise, effect, context, messages and channels, language and style, delivery, and ethics. It would help to review these and see if your students remember them. How do they specifically apply to public communication?

2. This unit details style and delivery in public speaking. It provides many examples for clarity. Starting on page 343, the author provides clarity guidelines. This is crucial because students generally have trouble with clarity. You will find the coverage helpful. Have students practice clear and unclear expressions.

3. Have students take the "Self-Test" on page 343. Distinguishing commonly confused words in English helps all students.

4. The "Media Watch" box on page 357 is about how we influence the media which provides another role for us as responsible citizens.

Thought Questions. *Thought-provoking questions for interesting discussions and assignments*

1. What does the author recommend as the preferred method of delivering public speeches? Why?
   A: DeVito recommends the extemporaneous method because it is most conversational allows more flexibility to feedback and interaction.

2. What parts of the extemporaneous speech delivery is it recommended that you memorize? Why?
   A: Memorize the first few sentences, the main points and the order in which they will be presented, and the last few sentences in order to achieve the ultimate effectiveness.

3. Why is the use of pause so important for effective delivery.

   A: The use of pause signals a transition between major parts of the speech; allows the audience time to think, digest, and ponder a rhetorical question; signals the approach of a particularly important idea.

4. What are some bodily actions that you can consciously use to make your speech more effective?

   A: Some bodily actions include eye contact, expressive face, commanding posture, natural gesturing, and movement.

5. Let's discuss methods of rehearsing your speech to maximize your performance. What helps you when rehearsing?

   A: Students' individual responses. Focus on timing the speech; perfecting your volume, rate, and pitch; incorporating pauses and delivery notes; perfecting your bodily actions.

6. What are the guidelines for producing a good outline?

   A: See pages 335-342.

UNIT 18: THE INFORMATIVE SPEECH

Unit Goals. *After completing this unit, you should be able to:*

- explain the principles of informative speaking

- define and identify the strategies for developing the speech of description

- define and identify the strategies for developing a speech of definition

- define and identify the strategies for developing the speech of demonstration

- analyze a speech according to the principles for informative speaking

Instructor Focus. *Helpful hints on what to focus on in this unit*

1. This unit talks about the basic principles of informative speeches and provides an excellent foundation for students preparing a speech. Review the principles.

2. The principles of informative communication are excellent and provide good advice. You might have to translate them slightly. Have groups explain one principle each. Ask: Why are these principles important? How will they help us in public speaking?

3. In the section on "Media Watch" on page 366, the knowledge hypothesis is addressed. Help the class interpret income and culture factors. Ask their opinion about reducing the knowledge gap. Have them explain their views.

4. Several strategies for defining are provided. Have the students write out definitions by etymology, by authority, by negation, and by direct symbolization.

Thought Questions. *Thought-provoking questions for interesting discussions and assignments*

1. Identify and explain the principles of informative speaking.
    A: The principles are: limit the amount of information, adjust the level of complexity, stress relevance and usefulness, relate new information to old, and vary the levels of abstraction.

2. What does it mean to combine high abstraction with specifics? Provide examples in answer this question.
    A: Students' individual responses.

3. Why are audiovisual aids helpful in informative public speaking?
    A: Review Unit 16.

UNIT 19: THE PERSUASIVE SPEECH

Unit Goals. *After completing this unit, you should be able to:*

- define and distinguish questions of fact, value, and policy

- explain the principles of persuasion: selective exposure, cultural difference, audience participation, inoculation, magnitude of change, identification, consistency, logos, pathos, and ethos

- define and explain the strategies for developing the speech to strengthen or change attitudes or beliefs

- define and explain the strategies for developing the speech to stimulate action

- analyze a speech according to the principles of persuasion

Instructor Focus. *Helpful hints on what to focus on in this unit*

1. This unit talks about the basic principles of persuasive speeches. It provides an excellent foundation for students preparing a speech. Review the principles.

2. The strategies of persuasive communication are excellent and provide good advice. You might have to translate them slightly. Have groups explain one principle each. Ask: Why are these principles important? How will they help us in public speaking?

3. Relate questions of fact, value, and policy to each other. Detail the differences. Have students identify examples you provide.

4. On page 381, the "Media Watch" box also talks about credibility. There's a news credibility scale which is fun to complete.

5. Explain the principle of inoculation. Have students give examples from their experience.

6. Have students compare and contrast the foot-in-the-door technique with the door-in-the-face technique. They should illustrate each in a practical way. Have them dramatize each.

7. The three proofs are the foundation for all rhetoric or speech - logos, pathos, ethos. Help students translate these phrases into meaningful statements with which they can identify.

8. There is a "Self-Test" on pages 391-392 which measures the student's credibility. Ask students if the test was valid for them. Do they see things differently or unequally?

9. Have the students take the Machiavellian "Self-Test" on page 397. Get their personal reactions to their scores.

Thought Questions. *Thought-provoking questions for interesting discussions and activities*

1. Generate questions of fact, value, and policy.
   A: Students' individual responses.

2. Demonstrate the persuasive strategies of glittering generality and attack.
   A: Students' individual responses.

3. Identify a topic on which you have exhibited the selective exposure principle. Explain first.
   A: Students' individual responses.

4. Can you think of an example of one of the motive appeals that has occurred in your life? Who has an example?
   A: Students' individual responses. The appeals include: fear; power, control, and influence; self-esteem and approval; achievement; and financial gain. Examples are encouraged - advertisements, interpersonal relationships, jobs, and family.

5. What are the strategies for strengthening or changing attitudes, beliefs, and values?
   A: Estimate your listeners' attitudes, beliefs, and values; seek small changes; demonstrate your credibility; and give listeners good reasons.

6. Why do we as human being resist change?
   A: We want to keep things basically the same; in order to change, we require good reasons from people we believe.

LEARNING BY DOING

UNIT ONE: PRELIMINARIES TO HUMAN COMMUNICATION

Activity One: Drawing a Model
Drawing a model of human communication will help students to apply the terms of the Elements of Communication model (Figure 1.2).

Objective. To apply the Elements of Communication (Figure 1.1) to the five areas of communication

Time. Approximately 20 minutes, or can be extended to 50 minutes

Group Size. Small groups of 3-4 each; must have seven different groups

Description of Activity. Divide the class into five groups. Each group will be assigned one of the five areas of human communication: intrapersonal, interpersonal, small group, public, and mass.

Groups are assigned the task of discovering the differences in the process of communication for their area. The focus should be on identifying the sender, the message direction, the channel(s), the receiver, and the feedback. Reference should be made to Figure 1.2, the Elements of Human Communication diagram.

The final product should be a drawing depicting their area of human communication. For example, a visual representation of the sender, the message, the channel, the receiver, and the feedback should be simply and creatively designed (stick figures, shapes, arrows, and labels). A representative from each group will explain what the group has created.

Some ideas might include designing a mobile, a creative drawing, a cartoon, or a metaphorical drawing.

Instructor Focus. Focus on guiding the students to specifically illustrate the five areas of human communication. Differences are highlighted in Table 1.1; encourage students to visually depict the information explained in Table 1.1.

Activity Two: Deal-a-Dimension
This exercise seeks to involve everyone in the class to create examples of how the four contexts of communication affect the overall process.

Objective. To apply the four contexts of communication (physical, cultural, social-psychological and temporal) to a single communicative event in an attempt to understand their impact

Time. 50 minutes

Group Size. Small groups of four each

Description of Activity. Divide the class into groups of four. Each group will be given one index card from three separate "Communication Context" piles labeled "Physical Dimension," "Cultural Dimension," "Social-Psychological Dimension," and "Temporal Dimension."

The physical context cards could include:
- classroom
- bowling alley
- bar
- park
- funeral parlor
- hospital
- restaurant
- church or synagogue

The cultural context cards could include:
- Hispanic females
- Nigerian males
- gay American males
- women between 40 and 45 years of age
- men between the ages of 25 and 30
- deaf children
- male and female inmates
- millionaires

The social-psychological dimension cards could include:
- young lovers
- grandma and grandpa with grandchildren
- married couple of 30 years
- a meeting of a student government group in conflict
- a baby's first birthday
- two people from two different cultures (Japanese and American)
- an ill student meeting with a professor
- a police officer giving you a ticket

The temporal dimension cards could include:
- morning
- evening
- 5:30 p.m.
- 1990
- 1968

- your birthday
- Halloween night

The group will create a dialogue which can best illustrate how all the chosen dimensions come into play. For example, if young lovers at a restaurant in 1951 are the chosen contexts, what might the dialogue be. Each context will influence the content of the message.

Students will then present their dialogues to the class. The class observers should then identify the obvious impact of each context on the process of communication.

Instructor Focus. Keep asking the question, "How does this context influence the content of the message?" The goal is to identify how the context influences the content of the messages we send.

Activity Three: Purposeful Finds
This activity involves individual assignments for each class member to bring in examples of the purposes of communication.

Objective. To apply the purposes of communication to existing areas and types of communication

Time. To be assigned 1-2 days in advance of class presentation; allow for one five-minute selection of "tasks" on a given day and 30 minutes of presentations on the assignment due date - according to the class size

Group Size. Entire class with individual assignments

Description of Activity. The assignments below should be listed/indicated on notecards (3x5) or small sheets of paper which may be placed in a hat and chosen "grab-bag" style by class members.

After selecting a card, the assignment is for each student to find an example of one of the purposes of communication in the following categories. Each presenter will explain how the demonstrated item represents a particular purpose of communication.

Make up 3x5 notecards that the say the following; students will each select one:
- a meaningful greeting card
- your horoscope
- the sports page
- stock market analysis
- review of a movie
- letter to the editor
- taped recording of music
- comic strip

- play review
- car ad
- picture of a computer
- perfume ad
- datebook calendar
- fortune cookie
- crystal
- fiction book
- college text
- magazine
- a letter to a friend
- picture of yourself
- a vacation ad
- an IRS tax form

UNIT TWO: PRINCIPLES OF COMMUNICATION

Activity One: Pick a Personal Principle
Applying a given principle of communication to everyday life will increase a student's awareness in understanding the communication process.

Objective. To apply the principles of communication to personal interactions

Time. Approximately 35 to 50 minutes; allow for more time if individual presentations will be given

Group Size. Entire class

Description of Activity. The assignment can be completed in class on a given day or can be assigned to be due for the next class.

Each student in the class will choose one of the principles of communication. There will be obvious duplications which will lead to different applications. After choosing the individual principle of communication, each student will be assigned the task of analyzing a communication interaction which illustrates a real life application of the principle at work. For example: Communication is irreversible - Students may analyze an experience which describes a communication event which could not be withdrawn.

Three experiential strategies may be used at your discretion in completing this assignment. The three methods include: writing, speaking, and listening.

1) Students may write a reaction paper of one page which analyzes an interaction illustrating their principle. Emphasis should be placed on identifying or illustrating how the principle is inherent in the communication event.

2) Students may speak for five minutes on their personal principle interaction (i.e., talking about how the principle relates to their personal life).

3) After listening to the individual presentations, class members might analyze the principle in action. Alternative principles of application to the event could be discussed. (This assignment can serve to develop listening skills.)

Instructor Focus. This exercise will help students apply the principles of communication through analysis of a transaction in the communication mode of writing, speaking, or listening. Set up the parameters of the assignment with the underlying goal of applying the theory/principle to a real life situation. Continue to focus on having the student apply the principle asking, "How is your principle specifically illustrated in the communication interaction?"

Activity Two: I Wish I Never Said That!

This activity will promote an applied understanding of communication as an irreversible process. The exercise will emphasize how important it is to be careful of what we say.

Objective. To apply the principle the communication is irreversible in developing an understanding that we cannot withdraw what we say

Time. 45 minutes; 15 minutes for group processing and 30 minutes for group sharing

Group Size. Small groups of 3-4 each

Description of Activity. Divide the class into groups of 3-4 students. Each group of students will be assigned the task of developing situations which illustrate the principle that communication is irreversible.

Class members will be certain to respond when you suggest examples from the below list which can universally demonstrate the "wish I never said that" aspect of this principle at work.

1) "I'm sure I'll see you tonight at the party." (You never considered that the person might not have been invited.)

2) "I'm so excited that you're having a baby." (You never considered that the person might have just put on extra pounds.)

3) Upon noticing a person near a beauty salon, you say, "Oh, I see you're going to get your hair done." (You never considered that the person just exited the salon with his/her new style.)

Group members can choose one participant to share his/her experience. Class observers should have the chance to comment on how we can avoid these experiences.

Instructor Focus. Be certain to focus on having students understand that it is difficult to withdraw what has already been said. Students should be made aware of how important it is to think before you speak and that what we say does have an impact on the other person; it is a stimulus which can receive multiple reactions.

Activity Three: State Your Intentions

Applying the principles of communication to a single statement will help students understand the aspects of communication involved.

Objective. To understand the principles of communication

Time. 30 minutes

Group Size. Entire class

Description of Activity. The instructor should read those statements listed below making sure to communicate the feeling that is being conveyed in the voicing of the message. (Feelings are indicated in the parenthesis.) Students should be careful to listen for the way the message is stated rather than the words themselves.

Instructor should read these phrases:

(Yelling) John, shut the door, please!
A: Parent reprimanding child; authority with power over someone

(Requesting) John, shut the door, please.
A: Friend to friend, equal power

(Authoritatively, but friends) John, shut the door, please!
A: Friend trying to manipulate; friend seeking power through nonverbals

Students should then answer the following questions for each statement:
- Who is saying the statement?
- To whom is it being directed?
- What is the content meaning of the statement?
- What implications does the relationship give the message?

An alternative to this assignment is to have students create their own phrases on 3x5 cards. Volunteer students in the class would then have the opportunity to say the phrase and others could answer the above questions for each statement.

Instructor Focus. Focus on the principles of communication as they may apply to the students' answers.

UNIT THREE: PERCEPTION

Activity One: Name That Stereotype!
This exercise will promote an applied understanding of stereotypes in action as portrayal on television; it will emphasize the importance of distinguishing what is stereotypical from what is actual.

Objective. To emphasize the influence of stereotyping on human perception

Time. One class period

Group Size. One group for each television series viewed and discussed (four should do)

Description of Activity. Have students view "Friends," "Ally McBeal," "Home Improvement," "Just Shoot Me," "Frasier," or any other shows they choose. Have them view an episode of the show before coming to class. Break the class into (say) four groups - one for each show viewed. The students should identify the stereotypes portrayed on each show.

Discuss how the stereotype influences their perception. Allow 20-30 minutes for the group discussion. Then, have each group summarize their decisions to the class as a whole. Depending on time remaining, discuss the findings after each summarizes or after all do so.

Instructor Focus. Call attention to what is stereotypical of actual people and what would be an actual person. You might want to relate the stereotyping to the function of parasocial relationships and perception. Review "Media Watch" on page 191 on "Parasocial Relationships."

UNIT FOUR: LISTENING

Activity One: "Who's On First?"

This exercise is adapted from Abbott and Costello's famous baseball routine "Who's On First?"
The activity was conceived by Lynne Judd.

Source. Bud Abbott and Lou Costello - "Who's On First?"
 The Golden Age of Comedy, Volume 1
 Murray Hill Records
 One Park Avenue
 New York, NY 10016

Objective. To practice listening for information

Time. 40 minutes - 10 minutes to play the recording, five minutes to answer prepared questions; remaining time to replay recording and check answers

Group Size. Entire class; individual participation

Description of Activity. After the types of listening have been introduced, play the selection, "Who's On First?" for the class.

After the recording, ask the students to write down the names of the players according to their positions (you may ask these questions orally or you can create a written sheet of questions based on the answer model below). After the students answer the questions, you may wish to play the sketch again so that students can listen specifically for information they may have missed.

Instructor Focus. Students will have a tendency to focus on the enjoyment of the sketch rather than on listening for the information. By replaying the recording, students will increase their understanding of the importance of listening for information.

Questions and Answers for "Who's On First?"
1. Who is the Pitcher?
2. Who is the Catcher?
3. Who is the First Baseman?
4. Who is the Second Baseman?
5. Who is the Third Baseman?
6. Who is Shortstop?
7. Who is Center Field?
8. Who is Right Fielder?
9. Who is Left Fielder?

1. Pitcher - tomorrow
2. Catcher - today
3. First Baseman - who

4. Second Baseman - what
5. Third Baseman - I don't know
6. Shortstop - I don't give a darn
7. Center Fielder - because
8. Right Fielder - unknown
9. Left Fielder – why

Bonus. What is the name of the team?
A: Lou Costello Junior Youth Foundation Baseball Team

Activity Two: Logging Your Listening

This activity provides students with the opportunity to explore their personal listening weaknesses. This exercise was adopted from Ann Seidler, Montclair State College.

Objective. To identify weaknesses and begin applying strategies to improve listening effectiveness

Time. To be assigned 2-3 days in advance of class presentation; allow for 10 minute explanation of activity and 30 minutes of sharing

Group Size. To be done individually

Description of Activity. Instruct students to choose one twelve hour day in a given three day period (allowing for personal scheduling difficulties) for the "logging" of their listening.

At the end of each logged hour, estimate the number of minutes spent listening and indicate the type of listening experience in which you were a participant. After you monitor your listening time in each hour, note when and why you did not listen in each listening experience. As example is provided below:

8-9 a.m. - listened to radio talk show; tuned out when talk show host talked about statistics of crime in the city. I was too tired to think about anything other than my day.

After the daily listening logs are completed, discuss the findings in class. Question for discussion may include:
- What are some of the common reasons for tuning out?
- Specifically what made you "tune in?"
- Did you discover any of your personal positive listening behaviors? Any negative behaviors?

Instructor Focus. Focus on encouraging students to build self-awareness of their own listening skills. If possible, distribute 6x9 index cards large enough to log their finds and small enough to carry comfortably during the selected day.

Activity One: "Please Don't Hate Me"
The situation applies the understanding of self-disclosure to a real life situation.

Objective. To illustrate the influences and responses to self-disclosure

Time. One class session or 60 minutes

Group Size. Entire class as participants/observers including two role players

Description of Activity. Two students can role play the following situation. A narrator can read the background information for the situation. Note that both characters can be male or female.

Gerry: Twenty-year-old East Coast college coed whose parents own a vacation home in a ski resort in New England.

Chris: Twenty-year-old college coed who recently transferred to Gerry's college from the West Coast.

Background: The situation takes place in the late Autumn when Gerry has graciously invited Chris, a new classmate to spend the weekend at a family vacation home in Vermont as a gesture of friendship. Chris happily accepts the invitation feeling contented and once at the house, Chris is given a beautiful guest room decorated with Gerry's late grandmother's crafts and handmade quilt. On the first night, the change of hearty Fall weather catches Chris off guard. Taking notice of a space heater on the floor, Chris turns it on and goes back to sleep, and awakens in the early morning to the smell of smoke, and notices that the handmade quilt on the bed is not on the floor, but next to the heater - smoldering. Chris is careful to snuff out the ashes without waking anyone and returns to notice a large burn hole in the quilt. The next morning Chris makes the bed in the guest room, and is intent on not telling Gerry about the incident for fear of losing a new friend. At breakfast, Chris says nothing. Noticing that something is obviously wrong, Gerry says:

Gerry: What's the matter?

Chris: Why should anything be the matter?

Gerry: You haven't said a word all during breakfast.

Chris: So...

Gerry: We've talked so much this weekend that it's just - well - sort of funny to see you acting so quiet.

Chris: Well, there is something.

Gerry: Yes?

Chris: I think you'll be upset and I don't know how to tell you this, but something really terrible happened last night. I'm really sorry. You've been so nice to me and all. I feel so stupid about his.

Gerry: Are you all right?

Chris: Well, to tell you the truth, I was really cold last night and turned on the space heater. I went back to sleep and without realizing I turned it too high, I guess, and the next think I knew, there was smoke on the floor.

Gerry: You're telling me that the fire department came and I slept through the whole thing? Is that the whole big deal? At least you didn't burn up!

Chris: Well, that's not the whole thing. You see, there's - there's a large burn hole in the quilt your grandmother made and I am just sick about telling you. I mean you've been so nice to me and all. You're probably ready to say, "Why on earth did I ever start with this jerk in the first place?" I mean, I'm so sorry, I can't tell you how stupid I feel about ruining the quilt.

There is dead silence and then Gerry responds saying: _____

Students will then have the opportunity to respond to this situation by writing down their immediate response to the way in which they feel Gerry should respond.

Students should then consider the following questions for discussion at this point:
1. Why is Chris afraid to tell Gerry of the mishap?
2. What fear does Chris have about the disclosure?
3. Have you ever been afraid to tell someone something? Why? Explain.
4. How would you handle such a disclosure?

Instructor Focus. Students should concentrate on defending their answers with specific references to the factors surrounding self-disclosure.

Activity Two: Window Undressing
Drawing the Johari Window will help students understand self-awareness.

Objective. To apply the Johari Window to understand our different selves

Time. One hour

Group Size. Entire class; individual work

Description of Activity. This writing exercise should be assigned after discussing the Johari Window in class. Once the class understands what information is appropriate for each quadrant, instruct the students to draw one Johari Window representing a significant other in their life.

Examples might include:
- boyfriend/girlfriend
- mother/father
- sister/brother
- best friend
- instructor
- employer

Instruct students to visualize the entire window as being of constant size, with the size of each pane being the variable; sometimes small, sometimes large. Students are to vary the size of the window according to their own self awareness in their chosen relationship.

The reaction paper should focus on the following questions:
1. What were you able to discover about yourself by analyzing the open areas in each relationship? The closed areas?
2. What information about self-disclosure is not indicated in the window?
3. What are the reasons that you might disclose to one person and not another
4. What are the rewards of disclosing? Can you detect any barriers to disclosing with this person?

Instructor Focus. Encourage students to understand that the relative size of a window indicated by a relationship can change according to our moods, our relationship and the subject matter, i.e., students should not get caught up in the "rightness" or "wrongness" of their answers. Explain your evaluation process for the writing assignment.

ACTIVITY THREE: OPENING YOUR WINDOW

Objective. To apply the Johari Window to understanding levels of self-disclosure
Time. 60 minutes

Group Size. Entire class; individual work

Description of Activity. Students should list 3-5 pieces of information in the following categories: open self, blind self, and hidden self following the example given below.

Open Self	Blind Self	Hidden Self
	things people have told you	fear of flying
male	that you didn't know before	insecurity
	(i.e., good writer, easy to be	indecisiveness
	with	

Identify the kinds of information listed: facts, ideas or thoughts, feelings/emotions, or secrets. For example: Write a one page reaction paper explaining what you've learned about your levels and types of disclosure.

Instructor Focus. Instruct students to concentrate on specifically applying the factors that influence self-disclosing communication to their discussion.

UNIT 6: CULTURE AND COMMUNICATION

Activity One: A Personal Effectiveness Journal Entry
This exercise will help students recognize and apply effective principles of intercultural communication to their own lives.

Objective. To discover personal examples that illustrate principles of effectiveness in intercultural communication

Time. One week to complete assignment; one class period (50 minutes) to hear examples

Group Size. Whole class; done individually

Description of Activity. Briefly review the principles of effective intercultural communication, explaining each. Also review the journal writing criteria as used in past assignments.

Assign students to discover and write about an experience in their lives that illustrates each of the principles of effective intercultural communication (see pages 98-104). After a one-week period, students will select their favorite or most poignant examples to share with the class informally.

Here's an example:
Immediacy. The other day I was looking for a particularly important spice and went into a new ethnic food store. As I was browsing, a sales clerk, who was ethnically different, came over and was very friendly and helpful. He/She seemed very interested in helping me find just the right spice and even went out of his/her way to call other branches. I felt a sense of sincerity and genuine feeling of warmth through the clerk's smile, eye contact and personal reference to me by name. Although there were other customers in the store, this clerk gave me his/her undivided attention. It made me want to shop there again - and I will.

Instructor Focus. As with other journal entries, be certain that the student applies the intercultural concepts to the experience.

UNIT SEVEN: VERBAL MESSAGES

Activity One: The Great Pretenders
This exercise will enable students to recognize the disadvantages of lying.

Objective. To understand lies and how they impact upon a person's credibility

Time. To be assigned 1-2 days before; 50 minutes during class

Group Size. Entire class; may be assigned individually or in groups

Description of Activity. Students should look around their own rooms for objects whose functions are not immediately known. Instruct students to consider utilizing parts of known objects such as a screw-in piece of a more complicated object or a piece of an assembled item. Other possibilities can include photos, keys, or unlabeled bottles.

On the due day of the assignment, students should make up a story about their objects OR tell the real truth and purpose of their object. The observers in the class can then vote as to whether the person is telling the truth or lying by evaluating the consistency of the communication package.

Instructor Focus. As a result of this exercise, students will get a first-hand experience in understanding the cues which affect credibility. Encourage students to closely watch and listen to presenters when presenting their own make up or true story. Focus on isolating the nonverbal and verbal consistency which betrays the communication package. Does the verbal message match the nonverbal cues? Are they congruent?

Activity Two: Busy Bodies
This exercise will help students to identify unethical kinds of gossip in their own lives.

Objective. To understand the problems of gossip

Time. 25 minutes

Group Size. Triads

Description of Activity. Divide the class into groups of three. The list below may serve as a springboard for gossip-related choices for students in each group.

1. family gossip
2. friendship gossip
3. boyfriend/girlfriend gossip
4. political gossip
5. community gossip
6. school-related gossip

Each group will be assigned the task of discussing a specific form of gossip which was evidenced in their own personal lives. Each group should choose what they believe to be the form of gossip which had the most serious problems in terms of ethical implications.

Group discussion should center on:
1. Why was the gossip managed incorrectly?
2. What are some of the effects of the unethical management of the information that was presented in the gossip?

An alternative to this assignment could be to assign students to write or present their own personal "principle of confidentiality" after their group discussions.

Instructor Focus. Alert students not to "gossip" about their gossip while in their small groups. Students should be instructed to focus on the implications of the gossip, rather than the gossip itself.

Activity Three: Ready, Set, Respond!
This exercise will helps students become actively aware of the difference between confirmation and disconfirmation.

Objective. To apply the differences between confirmation and disconfirmation to role playing situations

Time. One hour; 15 minutes to prepare role play response; 45 minutes of presentations and discussions

Group Size. Entire class divided into small groups of 3-4

Description of Activity. Divide the class into at least six groups. Each group will be assigned one of the situations described below. Students in each group decide whether they will role play a confirming or disconfirming response to the situation assigned to them. Discussion questions listed after the role play suggestions can serve as a follow-up to the activity. Reference should be made to pages 112-114 on confirmation versus disconfirmation. Focus should be placed on applying the information to role play which demonstrates confirmation or disconfirmation. Observers will then guess if the role played response was confirming or disconfirming.

The role play situations, written on index cards, may be assigned or randomly chosen by students. If the class is large, students may be assigned the same situation which will add to the understanding of different applications of confirmation and disconfirmation.

1. Senior student A wants to tell Senior student B how he/she feels about not finding a job after graduation. Student A is trying to sound as if nothing is really wrong and ways, "Well, I guess I'm not the only one out of work." Student B responds:

2. Professor A questions student B about his/her attendance. Student B replies that there was an extenuating circumstance which necessitated the absences. Professor A responds:

3. Person A starts to tell person B that he/she is no longer interested in dating him/her. Person A begins by saying, "I think that we need to start seeing other people - to sort of test our feelings for each other." Person B responds:

4. Parent A indicates to college son/daughter that he/she is not spending enough time at home. Son/daughter responds:

5. Employer A wishes to share the results of an evaluation with employee B. A calls B into the office and says, "This evaluation is the first of many, I'm sure." B responds:

6. Friend A has just had a horrible date and calls friend B to talk about the evening. Friend B is just about to leave the house when the phone rings. B responds:

Some discussion questions could include:
1. Identify any confirmation/disconfirmation patterns that you may have developed which may impair your relationships.
2. How can your knowledge of confirmation and disconfirmation allow you to better understand your own communication style?
3. What types of observations have you made from the role plays?

Instructor Focus. Students should be encouraged to role play the scene briefly in a designated time frame which does not exceed 3-5 minutes. One student in each group should introduce the situation so that observers can better understand the role play.

UNIT EIGHT: NONVERBAL MESSAGES

Activity One: Demonstrating Nonverbal Messages

Objective. To understand the six categories of nonverbal messages

Time. One class period or slightly less

Group Size. The entire class divided into six equal groups

Description of Activity. Students will display one of the six ways that nonverbal messages interact with verbal messages by demonstrating them to the class. After dividing the class into six equal groups, assign each group one of the six categories of nonverbal messages: accenting, complementing, contradicting, regulating, repeating, and substituting. The group is responsible for creating a realistic illustration of their assigned category. They may want to select at least three examples. Give the groups about 10 minutes to play and then have each group demonstrate the same examples without the nonverbal component and see if the message has the same meaning.

Activity Two: Communicating Without Vocalizing
This activity will help students focus on a planned use of nonverbal behaviors (primarily gestures, facial expression, and posture).

Objective. To identify the meanings communicated through the use of gestures, facial expression, and posture

Time. 50 minutes; 10 minutes for the first exercise, 40 minutes for follow-up

Group Size. Entire class with four students selected to perform

Description of Activity. Select four students, two to study conversation #1 and two to study conversation #2, as they appear below. Each dyad will present the conversation nonverbally to the class. Observers will observe and comment on how meaning was derived from the use of nonverbal communication behaviors.

To follow-up on this assignment, instruct students to create their own gesture monologue and present their own work to the class the next class period.

Conversations without vocalization:
#1   A: Come here.
       B: Who, me?
       A: Yes, you!
       B: No! I'm sick.
       A: I'm waiting!
       B: No! I'm nervous.

A: Come here, I'm angry!
B: Go away!

#2   C: Stop it!
D: What?
C: You know.
D: No, I don't understand.
C: You make me so mad.
D: I'm sorry.

Instructor Focus. Students in the first exercise should be encouraged to use appropriate emblems that create the meaning of the verbal conversation. Overstated gestures should be discouraged.

Activity Three: The "Eyes" Have It!
This exercise will help students become more aware of their eye movements and expressions.

Objective. To practice the functions of eye communication

Time. 20 minutes

Group Size. Entire class divided into dyads

Description of Activity. Divide the class into dyads. Students should be instructed to sit face to face. One person should be "A," the other "B." Each dyad should be given the set of instructions below. Instructor will need to create 10-15 sets of "A" and "B" cards to distribute to each dyad.

Person "A" will try to guess what person "B" is communicating through his/her eyes (use one had to cover mouth). One each "A" and "B" card, write: "Use your eyes to communicate the following:"

Person A
1. Express "no"
2. Express interest in the other person
3. Indicate that the other person should start talking
4. Express anger
5. Express understanding
6. Express boredom

Person B
1. Express "yes"
2. Express disinterest in the other person
3. Indicate that the other person should stop speaking
4. Express happiness

72

5. Express lack of understanding
6. Express surprise

After person "A" expresses the assigned eye communication, person "B" in each dyad will indicate what expression or idea was communicated. If the answer is incorrect, person "A" will try again. Person "B" will then follow suit.

An addition to this exercise could be to have students add facial expressions to help convey the message. Students can indicate the difference that facial expressions make.

Instructor Focus. Some of the eye movements expressing these different relationships and ideas are so similar, we often utilize information from other areas, particularly the face, to decode the message before making final judgment. It will be easier when adding facial expression.

Activity Four: Emotions Overrule!
This activity will develop an understanding of facial expression, body and eyes convey emotion.

Objective. To explore the way in which body, face, and eyes communicate meaning

Time. Approximately 50 minutes - 25 minutes for groups to prepare and five minutes for each group presentation

Group Size. Entire class divided into groups of 3-4

Description of Activity. This exercise will be played like the game "Charades" except members will be divided into teams of approximately four members each. Each team will work on a scene together. They will try to represent an emotion or emotional characteristic within the context of a scene. This scene will be absent of dialogue, and thus performed nonverbally not pantomimed. While one group is acting out the scene, the other groups will watch silently and then write down what they feel happened and the primary emotion involved.

The following emotions can be assigned to each group, or groups may chose to reenact their own emotion or emotional characteristic.
1. horror
2. fright
3. delight
4. boredom
5. sorrow
6. depression
7. exultation
8. flirtation
9. arrogance
10. anger
11. jealousy
12. surprise

Instructor Focus. Students should be directed to concentrate on nonverbally illustrating how the body communicates emotion.

Activity Five: Seat Changing

Source. D. Malamud and S. Machover, Toward Self Understanding: Group Techniques in Self Confrontation

Objective. To understand the concept of territoriality

Time. 30 minutes

Group Size. Entire class

Description of Activity. Begin the activity by verbalizing that some members tend to take certain fixed seats each week while others tend to sit in different seats from session to session. Then suggest that each member pick a seat as different as possible from his/her present one.

At your signal, class members should get up and change their seats. You should also change your seat. When the class has finished the seat changing, ask what they observed and experienced as they went about the task. The discussion which follows may touch on such aspects of the experience as the following: the resistance to or eagerness for change, the wish to sit or not to sit next to a specific member, indecisiveness about where to sit, competitiveness for particular places, how the room looks from the new position, the reaction to the leader's new seating position.

Questions for discussion:
1. To what degree is your new seat different from your old one?
2. Who thought of sitting in the leader's chair? On the arm of the chair? On the table? On the floor?
3. How does it feel not to have your same seat?

After discussion, ask the group to return to their old seats, and once they have done this, ask them for their reactions to this new change. Some students will prefer to stay in the new seats, but will comply with the instructor's instructions to return to the old seat.

Instructor Focus. Students should be encouraged to focus on the concept of territoriality in response to their feelings about this exercise. Although other issues will develop in the post-activity discussion, direct students to refer to specific aspects of territorial encroachment.

Activity Six: Reach Out and Touch Someone
This exercise will help develop an awareness of our reaction to touching people we do not know well, as well as being touched by these people.

Objective. To explore the touch avoidance behaviors

Time. 30 minutes

Group Size. Entire class

Description of Activity. One person is blindfolded and the rest of the group forms a circle around that person. One member of the circle should be directed to go forward to allow the blindfolded person to touch him/her, and thereby identify him/her. Only five "touches" are allowed.

Students should focus on the following observations:
1. Does the toucher touch hesitantly or confidently?
2. How do we recognize each other? By clothes? By physical features?
3. How does the touched person react? Tense? Ticklish?
4. Are our feelings about being touched cultural or personal?

Instructor Focus. This exercise works best with a small group of students. You may decide to have two circles with a large group so that each student may have a turn. Responses to the activity can also be written in the students' journals or notebooks.

Activity Seven: Pulling It All Together
This exercise will increase students' understanding of space, territoriality, and touch communication.

Objective. To apply an understanding of the unit to real life situations

Time. Two days; 60 minutes of planning and 60 minutes of presentations/discussion

Group Size. Entire class; six groups of three or more students

Description of Activity. Create six groups of 3-4. Each group will be assigned one of the following:

1. spatial distances
2. influences on space communication
3. territorial invasion
4. reactions to territorial invasion
5. the ways we use markers
6. the meanings of touch

Each group will create brief "skits" to demonstrate and illustrate the concepts of the section which they were assigned.

For example, Group One with the spatial distances could create different distances. (A brief introduction or concluding statement by a group member could elucidate on the content of the section which the group illustrated.)

Instructor Focus. Students should understand the unit prior to working on these exercises. Learning By Doing exercises utilized in other activities may help create ideas for this activity.

Activity One: "Hannity and Colmes" vs. "The Crier Report"
The exercise will help students understand the complexities of maintaining conversations.

Objective. To discover a variety of ways to signal conversational turns

Time. One class period

Group Size. Entire class

Description of Activity. Have the students view each show. One segment from each would suffice. Viewing the entire show for each would provide a clear sample.

The students should view the shows paying special attention to conversational cues (see pages 156-158). In class, "The Crier Report" should be analyzed through these conversation cues; then, "Hannity and Colmes" can be analyzed likewise. The two shows can then be assessed from the point of view of conversational turn cues.

Instructor Focus. Call attention to the extremely different styles of signaling conversation turns that each show practices. Ask students which style they prefer and why they prefer it.

UNIT TEN: INTERPERSONAL RELATIONSHIPS

Activity One: The World's A Stage
A closer look at the six stages of a relationship will provide students with a greater understanding of relationship development and deterioration.

Objective. To demonstrate the five stages of a relationship

Time. One class period (50 minutes)

Group Size. 10 volunteers, five groups of two to role play; entire class participation and observation

Description of Activity. Choose 10 volunteers and divide them into five groups of two. Each dyad will role play one of the five stages of a particular relationship: contact, involvement, intimacy, deterioration, and dissolution. Students may choose to role play one of the relationships below:

1. boyfriend/girlfriend
2. husband/wife
3. friend/friend (male-female)
4. friend/friend (male-male or female-female)

Participants must role play a different stage of the SAME relationship, and should present their skits in sequence (i.e., intimacy would follow involvement and precede deterioration). Five to eight minutes should be allotted for each skit.

Class members not participating in the skits should list all observations they made about each stage.

Post-activity discussion should focus on the following:
1. What characteristics were inherent to a given stage?
2. What factors led to intimacy in the relationship? To deterioration?
3. What may happen if one or more of the stages is skipped or out of sequence?

Instructor Focus. Review the five stages of relationships with the class before completing this exercise. Participants role playing may need to accentuate the primary qualities of that stage in order to highlight these qualities for the class.

Activity Two: So Nice To Meet You!

Objective. To illustrate the stages of nonverbal and verbal encounters to initiating relationships

Time. 50 minutes; 20 minutes group work and 30 minutes of presentation

Group Size. Entire class in groups of 3-5

Description of Activity. Review the aspects of both the nonverbal and verbal encounter with the class. Each small group should create a one page dialogue with nonverbal directions which illustrates a first meeting. Students should create their own settings and characters. Originality is stressed.

Instruct students to focus on the eight points illustrated in the nonverbal encounter and the seven points of the verbal encounter. Notations can be indicated in the margin of each group's dialogue for the purposes of noting how each point is applied.

The dialogue can then be presented informally to the class. Group members can follow this by discussing their first encounters.

Instructor Focus. Stress the 20 minute preparation time, otherwise students may be tempted to write a lengthy screen play! The focus should be on illustrating nonverbal and verbal aspects of the first encounter.

Activity Three: Breaking Up Is Hard To Do
This exercise will increase the awareness of students of the process involved in relationship deterioration.

Objective. To help students understand the communication changes that take place during the relationship deterioration

Time. One hour plus; may require two class periods

Group Size. Small groups of three

Description of Activity. Divide the class into groups of three. Distribute a handout to each group with the following examples of relationships that are in the deterioration stage. Instruct each group to choose a situation (or assign to the group). Allow each group to plan an information improvisation which will ultimately terminate the relationship.

Situational Examples of Relationship Deterioration - Improvisationally role play the termination of the relationship in one of the following situations:

1. A cohabiting couple constantly argues over financial matters. Both people in the relationship become ill at ease with each other concerning issues of money which results in the deterioration of the relationship. Person A tells person B, "I can't stand it anymore! I'm paying for everything around here!"

2. An employer finds it necessary to fire an employee who is not working up to his/her ability. The employee has not consented to remain in the office overtime and has recently been observed making copies of accounts of files for what appears to be for his/her personal use.

The employer confronts the employee by saying, "It's become increasingly obvious that you are not happy here."

3. A boyfriend/girlfriend is tiring of his/her involvement in an intimate relationship and wants to begin dating another. Person A says, "I need more space."

4. Two friends who were once inseparable constantly argue about infringing on each other's privacy. One friend finds the other reading his/her personal mail, and says, "Now you're into my mail. This is going too far!"

Instructor Focus. Give students an exact time limit in which to prepare and present their role plays. Focus on the deterioration process in the relationship in post-activity discussion.

Activity Four: Letting Go
This activity will help students focus on the reason for relationship deterioration.

Objective. To understand the nature of relationship deterioration

Time. 50 minutes

Group Size. Entire class; individually assigned

Description of Activity. Students should be instructed to bring their address books to class on a given day. Ask students to consider which names each person would eliminate if a new address book were to be given to them.

Students may be divided into groups to discuss their feelings or students can be given the opportunity to place some of their thoughts about this activity in a written account which may focus on:
1. What are some of the thoughts that entered your mind when eliminating a person's name from your book?

2. What were the reasons for the relationship deteriorating?

3. Did you experience second thoughts about the name elimination?

4. Why do we sometimes refuse to let go?

Instructor Focus. If students cannot bring in address books, students may bring in photo albums and think about eliminating pictures.

UNIT ELEVEN: INTERPERSONAL CONFLICT

Activity One: Visual Images of Conflict Management
This exercise will help students recognize unproductive methods of conflict management.

Objective. To illustrate unproductive methods of conflict management

Time. 20 minutes

Group Size. At least five groups, preferably groups of three each

Description of Activity. Divide the class into groups as suggested above. Assign each group one of the unproductive methods of conflict management. Ask them to begin to visualize how their method would look in terms of body positions, facial expressions, gestures, posture, intensity, and space relationships.

Students will be assigned the task of visualizing their unproductive method of conflict management in a frozen-position tableau which best illustrates how the method "looks." The case below will serve as a conflict scene established. A headline or caption is written to characterize both the type of unproductive conflict management assigned and the picture created. The headline is written down and handed to the instructor who will read it as the tableau is presented to the class.

An example for the situation below might be: 1) the server pouring a glass of wine on person A's head while person B gasps in horror and person A screams (without sound). The headline might be "Force Used in Dinner Dilemma."

Read the following conflict to the class:
"Two people have gone out to dinner at a nice restaurant. Person A fails to get what he/she ordered. When person A does receive the order, it is undercooked. Person A makes a scene and embarrasses person B. The server is upset."

Give the groups five minutes to create their tableau and write their headline to describe visually the type of conflict they have been assigned. In other words, how would force as an unproductive conflict method look in the conflict scene above? Groups will present their tableaus to the class separately as the instructor reads the headline.

Instructor will point out the eight unproductive conflict management techniques as they are illustrated and could also ask for definitions of each.

Instructor Focus. Make sure the students can readily recognize these eight unproductive conflict management techniques.

Activity Two: Applied Conflict Management
This exercise will help students understand the importance of effective conflict management techniques.

Objective. To illustrate the effective strategies of conflict management

Time. One class period (50 minutes)

Group Size. Divide the class into at least five groups

Description of Activity. Each of the five groups is assigned one of the five guides to effective conflict management. A narrative case is read to the class with an unresolved conflict. Each group must then prepare an oral explanation or dialogue which solves the conflict according to their assigned guide.

Unresolved conflict (to be read to the class after instructions):
"Four roommates have been planning a big party to be given at their newly-decorated apartment on the following evening. One of the roommates recently discover that his/her parents are planning a last-minute visit to see the apartment; consequently, he/she requests that the party be canceled. The three other roommates refuse the request."

Instructor Focus. Focus specifically on the strategies of effective conflict management, rather than on the issue of who is right. Encourage students to write the dialogue rather than just explain the solution; this method will assist them in building the skills of effective conflict management.

UNIT TWELVE: INTERVIEWING

Activity One: Preparing Answers
This exercise will help students strengthen the communication skills necessary in the interview process.

Objective. To practice writing and delivering answers to interviewing questions

Time. 20 minutes

Group Size. Dyads

Description of Activity. Students will select a cross-section of ten questions from the list of question in the book under "Common Interview Questions." Students should have one or two days to prepare the answers.

Ask the students to select a partner and sit facing him/her on the due date of the assignment. Each student has his/her list of ten selected questions to be given to the partner. Students take turns asking their partners five randomly-chosen question from the interviewee's list. The interviewer will provide brief feedback about the effectiveness of the responses.

See page 232 for guidelines for effective answers. Use the suggestions given under the section entitled "Demonstrate Confidence."

Instructor Focus. Emphasize the "Demonstrate Confidence" suggestions above for the interviewers to provide feedback. Students should be encouraged to develop positive and purposeful responses. Review the criteria prior to the classroom experience.

Activity Two: Who Am I on Paper?
This exercise will help students develop a resume that is an appropriate representation of their skills and experience.

Objective. To create a brief resume

Time. One week

Group Size. Individual assignment

Description of Activity. Give the students one week to prepare the content of a one page personal resume. Begin by having students write all pertinent information related to the sample resume on page 228. Then they will type the selected information to match the format of the sample resume to create a finished product which they will hand into the instructor. Instructor will provide brief, written comments for each student.

Instructor Focus. Stress the importance of discovering the student's special competencies and the skills appropriate for the selected career focus. This assignment also allows the instructor to encourage students to discover various career opportunities and to select one focus.

Activity Three: Getting What You Want to Know
This exercise will help develop students' investigative skills for obtaining information.

Objective. To practice the skills involved in preparing for an informational interview

Time. One class period

Group Size. Individual assignment

Description of Activity. Have students choose one person (parent, friend, roommate, teacher) from whom they will discover the answer to the question, "How did you get to where you are today?" Students will prepare a list of eight questions, the answers to which will help them discover the specific information desired. One of the question may not be the above question. Emphasis should be placed on knowing what type of information the student wishes to elicit from the interviewee. Knowledge of the selected person should be considered when formulating the questions. The focus should be on the formulation of the questions. If time allows, students could be given the opportunity to complete this assignment by performing the actual interview. Students could also share valuable insights regarding their successes or difficulties in obtaining the information.

See pages 224-225 for the author's suggestion for guidelines for informational interviews.

Instructor Focus. Encourage students to sharpen their skills in phrasing questions that are concise and focused.

UNIT THIRTEEN: SMALL GROUP COMMUNICATION

Activity One: Formats in Review
Creating examples of each of the four small group formats will illustrate to the class the primary differences for each.

Objective. To understand the differences between the four major small group formats

Time. Two days of class time

Group Size. Entire class divided into four separate groups

Description of Activity. Divide the class into four separate groups, hopefully with five or six members per group. Assign each group one of the small group formats: 1) round table, 2) colloquy, 3) symposium, or 4) symposium-forum.

Each group will meet during the first class period to create a role play of what their format looks like in action. They will assign roles, create topics and information, and design the procedures to present to the entire class the next class period. Emphasize to the groups that the primary objective is to illustrate how each format works and looks rather than worry about specific content of the presentation. Encourage the use of characters and humor to liven up the presentations. For example, the colloquy group will create experts on a selected topic (i.e., Professor Hazelnut, an expert on rain forests; Robert Godfrey, president of the Earth Firsters to save the Earth; and James Winfield, a member of Greenpeace). A moderator (Phil Donahue) will "interview" these experts in front of a studio audience, who may ask questions of the experts or give opinions at the appropriate time through the moderator.

The instructor should meet with each group on the first day to help them formulate their presentation.

The second class period, each group will have 10-20 minutes to present their format which will be followed by a summary and discussion of that format led by the instructor.

Instructor Focus. Emphasis is on the accuracy of the procedures for each format, not the content. This assignment can be fun with some added creativity and humor for characters and topics.

Activity Two: Brainstorming
Practicing the process of brainstorming will reveal its benefits.

Objective. To demonstrate the benefits of brainstorming as a problem-solving technique

Time. One class period

Group Size. Entire class

Description of Activity. Instruct the class to brainstorm on the following top: ways to socialize that are inexpensive. Write down all the ideas that students come up with. There should be no judgment made regarding these answers. After 15 minutes, when suggestions have been exhausted, have students select their top five options. This selection should not be a random choice, but rather an exercise in prioritizing. After this selection has been made, have students vote for their number one inexpensive way to socialize. Their selection must be one of the five options previously selected, and there must be consensus among class members.

Instructor Focus. Review the two phases of brainstorming: generation of ideas without judgment and the evaluation period. Also review the four brainstorm rules. Focus on the process of brainstorming itself rather than the "rightness" or "wrongness" of individual answers.

UNIT FOURTEEN: MEMBERS AND LEADERS

Activity One: The Roles We Play
This exercise will demonstrate the three types of group roles taken on by individuals during group communication.

Objective. To identify the various roles that group members play during the small group communication process

Time. One class period (50 minutes) - 10 minutes for instructions and group formulation, 15-20 minutes for the simulation, 15-20 minutes for reports from observers

Group Size. Whole class

Description of Activity. Create two sets of 3x5 cards on which are written individual group member roles with a description of the task (i.e., initiator-contributor - presents new ideas or new perspective on old ideas) as described in the text on pages 261-262. Divide the class in half and label group one as role players and group two as observers. Now distribute one set of cards to group one and the other set to group two. Everyone should have one card; left over cards should match.

Members of group one will role play the member role on the card he/she receives; this group will form a circle in the middle of the room and discuss a poignant topic selected by the instructor to stimulate a group meeting (i.e., tuition increase, parking problems on campus, other relevant topics to which students can easily relate).

Members of group two will serve as observers in a circle surrounding the inner circle. These observers will seek to identify the person in the center circle who is enacting the member role on the observer's card. These observers will write down their observations and share them with the class at the end of the simulation.

For example: person A (role player in inner circle) receives the card "encourager" and will act out that role while participating in the simulated discussion. Person one (observer) receives the duplicate card "encourager" and will seek to identify which person in the inner circle is playing that member role.

Instructor Focus. While this exercise may seem complicated, the organization you provide will serve to create a lively, realistic experience in identifying group member roles. Using the participant observer format with a "fish bowl" approach allows students to actively demonstrate and observe their understanding of the concepts being studied.

An alternative or extension to this exercise is to have students actually observe (as a participant) a group, and identify as many roles as they can during one meeting. This exercise also could be done by having students call up an experience from a group experience they have had.

Activity Two: "Groupthink" - a video and discussion

There two versions of "Groupthink:" an early version and a recent version. Either will serve your educational needs.

Objective. To identify the eight symptoms of "groupthink" (see page 264)

Time. One class period (50 minutes)

Group Size. Whole class

Description of Activity. Order and show the video "Groupthink" to the class. Before the video begins, instruct the students to take notes. (The video clearly and visually identifies the eight symptoms of "groupthink" with an example for each. These eight symptoms are also in the text).

Following the video, lead a discussion on each of the eight symptoms, asking individual students to explain their understanding of the symptoms. Ask students to also relate a personal example that might illustrate the same.

Instructor Focus. Encourage students to verbalize their understanding of these symptoms through examples from the video or their personal experience. An alternative could be to have them write instead of speak.

UNIT FIFTEEN: TOPIC, AUDIENCE, AND RESEARCH

Activity One: A Dry Run
Going through the preparation of a speech will assist students in understanding the process.

Objective. To practice the process of preparing a speech

Time. 50 minutes

Group Size. Entire class together

Description of Activity. Announce that today you will, together as a class, go through the entire process of preparing a speech using the 10 steps highlighted on page 285 in the text. The topic is "Your Grocery Shopping List." Take the class through each step as you see fit to help them learn how to plan a speech.

Instructor Focus. Encourage class participation by asking what should be done next. Remember the order is not as important as the process. Follow whatever order seems logical and appropriate for the topic. The topic selected allows for easy organization (the use of topical pattern) through categories of food, research begins in your kitchen to see what you need, and the thesis can be to have a well-stocked kitchen for the week of classes which allows you to create logical support through specific food items necessary for certain meals. This exercise has proven to work very well.

UNIT SIXTEEN: SUPPORTING AND ORGANIZING YOUR SPEECH

Activity One: Create an Audiovisual
Making an audiovisual presentation aid will help students understand the methods and procedures to follow.

Objective. To learn how to make various types of audiovisual aids

Time. 30 minutes

Group Size. Entire class; individual assignment

Description of Activity. Students will be assigned the task of creating one audiovisual aid for a selected speech topic (either the instructor will select one topic for the class or perhaps the class is doing an informative speech and can use their own current topic). A good topic for everyone to do is "someone or something I feel strongly about," or demonstrate how to do or make something.

Students must select one type of audiovisual from Table 25.1 and can either create (draw or make) their own or bring in an already made one. Encourage a variety of types. If you sense everyone selecting the easy way out by making a simple poster, you might want to assign some of each type listed in Table 25.1. Students will present their audiovisual aid in front of the class explaining which functions it serves and what type it is.

Instructor Focus. If time allows, you may even want to assign an informative speech (2-4 minutes) and require at least one audiovisual aid. You might want to "approve" the aid prior to the speech as a learning evaluation. With any of the approaches to learning about these, focus on visual effectiveness.

Activity Two: Audiovisual Aids' "Bloopers"
Showing poor examples of audiovisual aids will enlighten students about what NOT to do:

Objective. To demonstrate the "pitfalls" of making audiovisual aids

Time. 20 minutes

Group Size. Entire class as participants/observers

Description of Activity. When explaining the different types of audiovisual aids, bring in an example of each type that will illustrate the problems to avoid. For examples, use the following chart:

Presentation Types/Media	Problems to Avoid
actual object	too small
models	too small/doesn't match idea
chalkboard	messy writing style/hard to read/takes too long
charts	too much information/hard to read
graphs	too small to read/too much detail
maps	too small
slides/pictures	too small/passing around the room/flimsy
records/tapes	not cued/inaudible/too soft/distorted

Other Problems to Avoid
misspelling
mixed styles of printing
colors too light to read (never use yellow)
too messy
crooked
not used at proper time
held upside down
talking to the aid
not holding it up long enough
holding it up too long/leaving it up throughout the speech
forgetting to use it

Instructor Focus. If you prefer you can take the "positive" approach to these examples by showing "good" examples instead of bad ones. We have had excellent success, however, with the "bad" examples. Students are easily convinced they do not want to make these simple errors after you have illustrated them to everyone. BE SURE to talk about what makes for a good aid after each "bad" examples to reinforce the positive.

Activity Three. Amplifying Material
Finding good examples of amplifying material is a good research project.

Objective. To research for good examples of amplifying materials

Time. 30 minutes

Group Size. Entire class; individual assignment

Description of Activity. Students will be assigned the task of researching to find an example/illustration or testimony. Again, either one overall topic for the class can be selected or have the class present a short informative speech (2-4 minutes) with required amplifying material.

As a class activity, students can bring in a sample and present it to class. This process is quick and easy. Students will announce a topic and then present their amplifying material.

Instructor Focus. One idea is to request that students bring in amplifying material for the abstract concept of "love," "freedom," or "friendship."

UNIT SEVENTEEN: STYLE AND DELIVERY IN PUBLIC SPEAKING

Activity One: My Favorite/Worst Movie Impromptu
This short impromptu speech will aid students in practicing outlining and organization. It also assists them in focusing.

Objective. To practice the skills of outlining and organizing

Time. 50 minutes for individual, one minute impromptus, with 10-12 minutes for everyone to prepare

Group Size. Entire class presenting individual one minute impromptus

Description of Activity. At the beginning of the class period, instruct the class to prepare a one minute impromptu speech on his/her favorite or least favorite movie. Then put on the board, the outline below which they must follow and have them write it on a 3x5 card or a sheet of notebook paper. This written outline will be turned in AFTER they present their impromptu. The impromptu will be evaluated strictly on two things: 1) "are there two clear points?" (these can be two good points, two bad points or one of each) and 2) "is there an introduction, body with two points, and conclusion?"

The sample outline must look like this:
I   Introduction
II   Body
         A.
         B.
III   Conclusion (write out)

Instructor Focus. This activity is easy and fun for the student even though they complain about an impromptu. Tell them to pretend that they are telling their best friend about the movie - only today it will be more clear and more organized. Do not let them prepare more than 12 minutes, because they will take all hour if you let them. Call on students at random to facilitate the process. If speakers begin to speak for more than one minute, create a hand signal to indicate time for them.

Activity Two: Listen and Learn
Observing a speaker on campus (or another location) allows students to outline what they have heard, thus practicing the skill of outlining.

Objective. To learn the skill of outlining a speech

Time. One week assignment or coordinated with a speaker on campus

Group Size. Entire class done individually

Description of Activity. Assign the class to attend a public speech (all the same speech is the most ideal) and to outline what the speaker says indicating which organizational patter he/she used - temporal, problem-solution, or topical. Discussion of their findings or personal evaluations of their outlines provides feedback for the activity.

An alternative is to bring in a taped speech and have them do this assignment in class. This works very well and is easier to control.

Instructor Focus. While the original activity explained is very valuable, the alternative is an excellent way to accomplish the same task. Frequently, what the students will notice, is that many speakers are not organized but instead, rather hard to follow. A short speech is best.

Activity Three: Bloopers
Demonstrating certain delivery problems will assist students in avoiding them.

Objective. To demonstrate some incorrect methods of delivery

Time. 30 minutes

Group Size. 14 volunteers with the remainder of the class observing

Description of Activity. Prepare 3x5 notecards containing the following "bloopers" in delivery:

1. speaking too slowly
2. speaking with inappropriate pauses
3. using audible pauses
4. speaking too fast
5. speaking with an annoying high pitch
6. using poor articulation
7. leaning on the podium
8. no eye contact
9. forced smile
10. swaying or shuffling feet
11. playing with ink pen/clicking
12. volume too loud
13. volume too soft

Ask for 14 volunteers to demonstrate the above "bloopers" in speech delivery. One by one, they will present an exaggerated version of the "blooper" from a pre-selected passage the instructor provides. Class observers should be able to easily identify the problems these delivery "bloopers" create for effective public speaking. Instructor summary of the correct version is essential.

Instructor Focus. Explain to volunteers (individually) what you really want them to demonstrate; brief instructions will assist in making the examples more poignant.

Activity Four: Impromptu Rehearsal
Experiencing another impromptu will assist students in developing stronger delivery skills.

Objective. Practicing effective delivery skills

Time. 50 minutes

Group Size. Entire class

Description of Activity. At the beginning of the class period, announce the topic and the goals. Give the students 10 minutes maximum for preparation. Then proceed with volunteers or by calling specific names.

Students will be rated on an evaluation sheet by instructor (and students, if desirable) on volume, rate, pitch, articulation, pauses, and bodily action. A seven point evaluation scale works well. A sample evaluation sheet might look like this:

	1	2	3	4	5	6	7
Volume							
Rate							
Pitch							
Articulation							
Pauses							
Bodily Action							

Instructor Focus. While organization is important, as mentioned, the primary focus this time is on effective delivery.

Activity Five: Great Song, But What is it Saying?
Using popular music illustrates articulation and pronunciation problems in first hearing.

Objective. To find examples that illustrate the problems with poor articulation and pronunciation

Time. 15 minutes

Group Size. Entire class as observers

Description of Activity. Select three popular songs that particularly illustrate poor articulation and/or pronunciation. Play a short passage from each selection and ask students to write down what they heard. Have a prepared copy of the actual words for your reference (use a song where the words are printed in the liner notes of a cassette or CD). After students offer their versions of what the words are, read them the exact wording as printed. Discussion concerning the importance of saying it clearly the first time will ensue.

Instructor Focus. Students may allude to their ability to understand these types of popular music, BUT the issue is what is received the FIRST time the words are heard.

UNIT EIGHTEEN: THE INFORMATIVE SPEECH

Activity One: Seeing is Believing
This exercise will apply informative speaking principles to an informative speech; it will allow students to compare theory with practice.

Objective. To demonstrate the link between the principles and practice of informative speaking

Time. One class period

Group Size. Entire class participation

Description of Activity. Assign students to attend a lecture or informative speech scheduled for your campus. The speech should be at least 20 minutes long. Review the principles of informative speaking that begin on page 363. Have the students use these principles as criteria for judging the lecture or informative speech. Spend one class period hearing students give an account of the speeches they heard. This exercise can also serve as a graded report for the critique of a speech.

Instructor Focus. Call attention to the subtleties in the five informative speaking principles. Discuss what degree of each principle should be present in the speech.

UNIT NINETEEN: THE PERSUASIVE SPEECH

Activity One: Do You Buy That?
This exercise will demonstrate the foot-in-the-door and door-in-the-face technique.

Objective. To get students to recognize how each technique can be effective

Time. One class period

Group Size. Entire class divided into two large groups

Description of Activity. Review the two techniques on page 387. Have half the class seek out examples of one technique and half, the other. In class, each group reports its findings. The instructor can serve as the judge of how accurately each group classified the technique. Each group can also serve as a jury for each other's findings. Political speeches, commercials, infomercials, sales speeches, and other promotionals may serve as source materials.

Instructor Focus. Call attention to the details of the persuasive speeches that led to their classification as one technique or the other.

CHAPTER 1 Preliminaries to Human Communication

MULTIPLE CHOICE. Choose the one alternative that best completes the statement or answers the question.

1) Feedback can be looked upon in terms of these important dimensions:
   A) immediate, highly critical, and usually monitored.
   B) volume, speed, and accuracy.
   C) immediate-delayed, supportive-judgmental and true-false.
   D) immediate-delayed, low-monitoring-high monitoring, critical-supportive, positive-negative, and person focused-message focused
   E) monitored, honest, and spontaneous.

   Answer: D
   Diff: 2   Page Ref: 13-14
   Skill: Interpretive

2) Communication takes place in a context that is
   A) psychological, social, and temporal.
   B) physical, social, and psychological.
   C) physical and psychological; social and temporal aspects are external to the communication context.
   D) social-psychological, physical, cultural, and temporal.
   E) mostly social.

   Answer: D
   Diff: 2   Page Ref: 10-12
   Skill: Factual

3) This refers to messages that open the channels of communication rather than communicate information and is a perfect example of feedforward.
   A) Credentialing
   B) A cognitive disclaimer
   C) Hedging
   D) Phattic communion
   E) Altercasting

   Answer: D
   Diff: 1   Page Ref: 15
   Skill: Factual

4) The social–psychological dimension of a communication context can include

   A) the temperature.

   B) the friendliness or unfriendliness of the situation.

   C) the tangible environment in which the communication takes place.

   D) the time.

   E) the rules and norms of the people communicating.

   Answer: B
   Diff: 2   *Page Ref: 11*
   Skill: Factual

5) Which of the following constitute the types of noise in communication?

   A) Physical, psychological, physiological, and semantic

   B) Inform, persuade, and entertain

   C) interpersonal, public, and mass

   D) Temporal, cultural, and physical

   Answer: A
   Diff: 2   *Page Ref: 16*
   Skill: Factual

6) Which of the following is the best example of ethical communication?

   A) An advertisement

   B) A political campaign

   C) A job interview

   D) A confession of truth

   E) Disciplining a child

   Answer: D
   Diff: 2   *Page Ref: 17*
   Skill: Applied

TRUE/FALSE. Write 'T' if the statement is true and 'F' if the statement is false.

1) Noise is a disturbance in communication that distorts the message either physically, physiologically, psychologically, or semantically.

   Answer: TRUE
   Diff: 2   *Page Ref: 16*
   Skill: Interpretive

2) Communication noise may be internal to either the speaker or listener as well as external to the speaker or listener.

   Answer: TRUE
   Diff: 1   *Page Ref: 16*
   Skill: Interpretive

3) Ethics is external to both speaker and hearer as well as to the communication act.

Answer: FALSE
Diff: 2   *Page Ref: 16–17*
Skill: Interpretive

4) Communication ethics is an integral part of every communication transaction.

Answer: TRUE
Diff: 1   *Page Ref: 16–17*
Skill: Factual

5) Of the five major areas of human communication, the one in which we participate at all times is public communication.

Answer: FALSE
Diff: 1   *Page Ref: 2–3*
Skill: Applied

6) For every communication act, there is some consequence.

Answer: TRUE
Diff: 1   *Page Ref: 16*
Skill: Interpretive

7) An example of altercasting in feedforward would be the phrase "Don't get the wrong idea--I'm not sexist, but . . ."

Answer: FALSE
Diff: 2   *Page Ref: 15*
Skill: Factual

8) It is probably best for a communicator to ignore feedback if it is not positive.

Answer: FALSE
Diff: 2   *Page Ref: 13–14*
Skill: Applied

CHAPTER 2   Principles of Human Communication

MULTIPLE CHOICE. Choose the one alternative that best completes the statement or answers the question.

1) When we talk of communication as transactional we mean all of the following EXCEPT

    A) communication is an ever-changing process.

    B) communication components are interrelated.

    C) communicators act on the basis of the present situation.

    D) communicators listening to the same message derive the same meaning.

Answer: D
Diff: 2   *Page Ref: 21-22*
Skill: Factual

2) Which of the following postulates of communication refers to being unable to avoid communicating in an interactional situation?

    A) Communication is inevitable.

    B) Communication is irreversible.

    C) Communication is a package of signals.

    D) Communication is a process of adjustment.

Answer: A
Diff: 2   *Page Ref: 21-24*
Skill: Factual

3) The person who verbally expresses interest in seeing us but who never makes direct eye contact is sending

    A) punctuated messages.

    B) contradictory messages.

    C) transactional messages.

    D) intrapersonal messages.

Answer: B
Diff: 2   *Page Ref: 25*
Skill: Applied

4) The content dimension deals with

    A) the relationship between the people involved in the communication transaction.

    B) the behavioral responses expected of individuals.

    C) the context in which the communication takes place.

    D) the motivations of the communicators.

Answer: B
Diff: 2   *Page Ref: 24-25*
Skill: Factual

5) The tendency to divide the various communication transactions into sequences of stimuli and responses is referred to as

   A) compartmentalization.

   B) departmentalization.

   C) punctuation.

   D) sequentation.

   Answer: C

   Diff: 2   *Page Ref: 26*

   Skill: Factual

6) The process of adjustment refers to

   A) each person learning the other person's system of signals.

   B) learning to live with failure or success.

   C) each person learning to care more for the other.

   D) understanding the relationship message instead of just the content messages.

   Answer: A

   Diff: 2   *Page Ref: 22–23*

   Skill: Applied

7) When two individuals mirror each other's behavior--when the behavior of one person serves as the stimulus for similar behavior in the other person--we refer to this relationship as a

   A) complementary relationship.

   B) symmetrical relationship.

   C) similarity relationship.

   D) parsimonious relationship.

   Answer: B

   Diff: 2   *Page Ref: 26–29*

   Skill: Interpretive

8) When Pat drinks, Chris drinks. The more Pat drinks, the more Chris drinks. This relationship is best described as

   A) complementary.

   B) symmetrical.

   C) double-binding.

   D) transactional.

   Answer: B

   Diff: 3   *Page Ref: 26–29*

   Skill: Applied

9) The inability to change the kind of relationship existing between oneself and another even though the individuals and numerous other variables have changed considered to be one of

A) transactional processing.

B) extreme rigidity.

C) static punctuation.

D) irreversible pathways.

Answer: B

Diff: 2   Page Ref: 22-24

Skill: Interpretive

10) When the differences between the parties are maximized in relationships, that type of relationship is known as

A) complementary.

B) symmetrical.

C) static.

D) irreversible.

Answer: A

Diff: 2   Page Ref: 26-29

Skill: Factual

TRUE/FALSE. Write 'T' if the statement is true and 'F' if the statement is false.

1) When we are in an interactional situation, we can decide to communicate or not to communicate.

Answer: FALSE

Diff: 2   Page Ref: 21-22

Skill: Interpretive

2) In an interactional situation, all behavior sends a message and has message value.

Answer: TRUE

Diff: 2   Page Ref: 21-23

Skill: Factual

3) Communication is a reversible process.

Answer: FALSE

Diff: 1   Page Ref: 30-31

Skill: Factual

4) Communication is inevitable in an interactional situation.

Answer: TRUE

Diff: 1   Page Ref: 30-31

Skill: Factual

5) In the analysis of communication, punctuation refers to the translation of oral into written communications.

Answer: FALSE
Diff: 1   *Page Ref: 26*
Skill: Interpretive

6) When the behavior of one person serves as the stimulus for different behavior in another person, their relationship is complementary.

Answer: TRUE
Diff: 2   *Page Ref: 26–29*
Skill: Interpretive

7) While symmetrical relationships are bad, complementary relationships are good.

Answer: FALSE
Diff: 2   *Page Ref: 26–29*
Skill: Applied

8) An older brother who refuses to recognize that his sister has grown up and is now capable of taking care of herself is demonstrating extremely rigid complementarity.

Answer: TRUE
Diff: 2   *Page Ref: 26–29*
Skill: Interpretive

CHAPTER 3   Perception

MULTIPLE CHOICE. Choose the one alternative that best completes the statement or answers the question.

1) The theory of primacy–recency refers to

   A) whether what is perceived first or last has greater effect.

   B) the order in which we perceive personal characteristics.

   C) our making predictions and then causing them to come true.

   D) our emphasizing what we need or want.

   Answer: A
   Diff: 2   Page Ref: 42–43
   Skill: Factual

2) Perceptual accentuation refers to all EXCEPT

   A) seeing what we expect to see.

   B) seeing what we want to see.

   C) seeing what we have seen in the past.

   D) seeing people we like as smarter than people we do not like.

   Answer: C
   Diff: 2   Page Ref: 42
   Skill: Interpretive

3) Perceptual accentuation refers to the process whereby

   A) we predict something and then make it come true.

   B) we attempt to maintain consistency or balance in our judgments.

   C) we see what we expect to see and want to see.

   D) we utilize our fixed impressions of groups to judge individuals.

   Answer: C
   Diff: 2   Page Ref: 42
   Skill: Factual

4) In Chinese, the qualities that make up *shi gu* are part of this for more Chinese than English speakers.

   A) closure

   B) implicit personality theory

   C) contrast

   D) attributional theory

   Answer: B
   Diff: 2   Page Ref: 40–41
   Skill: Interpretive

5) Consistency theory would make all of the following predictions EXCEPT

  A) we expect a person we like to like us.

  B) we expect a person we dislike to like us.

  C) we expect a person we dislike to dislike us.

  D) we expect a person we like to dislike a person we dislike.

Answer: B
Diff: 2   *Page Ref: 43–46*
Skill: Applied

6) Attribution theory is mainly concerned with

  A) tracing the historical origins of words.

  B) the explanation of behaviors, particularly the reasons or motivations for these behaviors.

  C) the ways in which relationships develop, are maintained and deteriorate.

  D) determining the truthfulness of messages.

Answer: B
Diff: 2   *Page Ref: 43–46*
Skill: Factual

7) When, in attempting to determine the causality of behavior, we ask, "Do other people behave in the same way as the person on whom we are focusing?", we are focusing on

  A) consensus.

  B) consistency.

  C) distinctiveness.

  D) self–reflexiveness.

Answer: A
Diff: 3   *Page Ref: 46*
Skill: Applied

8) In self–attribution we attempt to account for

  A) the ways in which we are perceived by others.

  B) the sources of interpersonal effectiveness.

  C) our own behaviors.

  D) the reasons our relationships develop or deteriorate.

Answer: C
Diff: 1   *Page Ref: 47–49*
Skill: Factual

9) John was fired from a job he began a few months ago. If we attribute his firing to internal causes, we will hold John responsible. Which factor is an internal cause?

A) high consensus
B) low consistency
C) high distinctiveness
D) high controllability

Answer: D
Diff: 3   *Page Ref: 45-49*
Skill: Applied

10) Which country is known for strong uncertainty avoidance?

A) Jamaica
B) Denmark
C) Greece
D) Ireland

Answer: C
Diff: 2   *Page Ref: 53-54*
Skill: Factual

TRUE/FALSE. Write 'T' if the statement is true and 'F' if the statement is false.

1) If we were able to analyze stimuli completely, we would be able to explain perceptual processes.

Answer: FALSE
Diff: 2   *Page Ref: 38-40*
Skill: Interpretive

2) Perception is primarily a passive process.

Answer: FALSE
Diff: 2   *Page Ref: 38-40*
Skill: Factual

3) The judgments that we make about other people are based solely on the behavior of the people.

Answer: FALSE
Diff: 1   *Page Ref: 38-40*
Skill: Interpretive

4) Research indicates that a person described first in positive qualities and then in negative qualities is perceived as more positive than a person described first in negative qualities and then in positive qualities.

Answer: TRUE
Diff: 2   *Page Ref: 40-41*
Skill: Interpretive

5) A clear example of the self-fulfilling prophecy is the pygmalion effect.

Answer: TRUE

Diff: 2   *Page Ref: 41–42*

Skill: Interpretive

6) Over attribution refers to attributing everything a person does to one or two obvious characteristics.

Answer: TRUE

Diff: 1   *Page Ref: 48–49*

Skill: Applied

7) Generally, people have a system of rules that tells them which characteristics of an individual go with which other characteristics.

Answer: TRUE

Diff: 2   *Page Ref: 40–44*

Skill: Interpretive

8) A sociological or psychological stereotype refers to a fixed impression of a group of people.

Answer: TRUE

Diff: 2   *Page Ref: 44–45*

Skill: Factual

9) Because perception is a complex process, it is important to examine how and why messages differ from the ones sent from "out there" to the messages that actually get to the brain.

Answer: TRUE

Diff: 1   *Page Ref: 38–40*

Skill: Factual

10) Communication and relational effectiveness depend in great part on your accuracy in interpersonal perception.

Answer: TRUE

Diff: 1   *Page Ref: 49–51*

Skill: Interpretive

11) We use the principle of CLOSURE when we note that some items (people, messages, etc.) are too different from each other to be part of the same perceptual organization.

Answer: FALSE

Diff: 1   *Page Ref: 42*

Skill: Applied

12) Generally, research shows that if we feel people are in control of negative behaviors, we will come to like them.

Answer: FALSE
Diff: 2   Page Ref: 47
Skill: Factual

CHAPTER 4   Listening

MULTIPLE CHOICE. Choose the one alternative that best completes the statement or answers the question.

1) The communication activity we spend the most time on is
   A) writing.
   B) reading.
   C) listening.
   D) talking.

   Answer: C
   Diff: 1   Page Ref: 58
   Skill: Factual

2) Listening may be defined as
   A) a passive process of receiving messages.
   B) an uncontrollable process of receiving aural stimuli.
   C) a five-part process.
   D) oral perception.

   Answer: C
   Diff: 1   Page Ref: 57
   Skill: Factual

3) To listen with empathy means to
   A) feel what the speaker feels.
   B) understand what the speaker means.
   C) listen with an open and unbiased mind.
   D) listen with a closed and biased mind.

   Answer: A
   Diff: 1   Page Ref: 66–67
   Skill: Factual

4) Active listening serves all of the following functions EXCEPT:
   A) that it enables the listener to check on the accuracy of his or her understanding of what the speaker said.
   B) that it enables the listener to express an evaluation of what the speaker said.
   C) that it stimulates the speaker to explore further his or her feelings and thoughts.
   D) that it allows the speaker to know that you acknowledge and accept his/her feelings.

   Answer: B
   Diff: 3   Page Ref: 69–70
   Skill: Interpretive

5) Among the techniques suggested for learning active listening are all of the following EXCEPT
   A) paraphrasing the speaker's thoughts.
   B) expressing understanding of the speaker's feelings.
   C) expressing an evaluation of the speaker's feelings and thoughts.
   D) asking questions.

   Answer: C
   Diff: 3   Page Ref: 69-70
   Skill: Interpretive

6) Effective listening increases all of the following EXCEPT
   A) your ability to acquire knowledge.
   B) your ability to resolve all disputes.
   C) your ability to gain social acceptance and popularity.
   D) your ability to influence the attitudes and behaviors of others.

   Answer: B
   Diff: 3   Page Ref: 66-70
   Skill: Interpretive

7) Passive listening
   A) is a powerful means for communicating acceptance.
   B) is a negative form of listening.
   C) denotes laziness.
   D) provides an unsupportive environment.

   Answer: A
   Diff: 1   Page Ref: 66
   Skill: Factual

8) Listening with empathy
   A) includes both nonjugdmental and critical responses.
   B) is the only way to understand another person's meaning fully.
   C) is an emotional interpretation of the literal message.
   D) sends back to the sender what you as listener thinks the speaker meant.

   Answer: B
   Diff: 1   Page Ref: 66
   Skill: Interpretive

TRUE/FALSE. Write 'T' if the statement is true and 'F' if the statement is false.

1) Contrary to popular conception, listening is more often a passive rather than an active process.

Answer: FALSE
Diff: 1   *Page Ref: 66–69*
Skill: Factual

2) Hearing and listening are essentially the same process.

Answer: FALSE
Diff: 1   *Page Ref: 57–59*
Skill: Interpretive

3) In listening to a speech, we should rehearse our questions or possible responses in our minds while the speaker is speaking.

Answer: FALSE
Diff: 1   *Page Ref: 63–65*
Skill: Interpretive

4) Unlike speaking and writing, listening ability cannot be improved significantly.

Answer: FALSE
Diff: 2   *Page Ref: 66–70*
Skill: Interpretive

5) We should stop listening when inappropriate expressions or hostile remarks are made in a conversation.

Answer: FALSE
Diff: 1   *Page Ref: 66–70*
Skill: Interpretive

6) We should follow essentially the same general principles of listening when listening for enjoyment, for information, or to help.

Answer: FALSE
Diff: 2   *Page Ref: 66–70*
Skill: Interpretive

7) Passive listening is something we should avoid at all times.

Answer: FALSE
Diff: 2   *Page Ref: 66–70*
Skill: Interpretive

8) Listening should always be nonjudgmental.

Answer: FALSE
Diff: 2   *Page Ref: 66–70*
Skill: Interpretive

9) If we are to listen effectively, we must learn to disregard the literal meaning of a message and concentrate on its deep or hidden meanings.

Answer: FALSE
Diff: 2   *Page Ref: 66–70*
Skill: Interpretive

10) In addition to paraphrasing the content and asking questions, active listening involves echoing the feelings you felt the speaker expressed or implied.

Answer: TRUE
Diff: 2   *Page Ref: 66–70*
Skill: Factual

CHAPTER 5   Self

MULTIPLE CHOICE. Choose the one alternative that best completes the statement or answers the question.

1) The Johari window contains divisions for the
   A) open, blind, hidden, and unknown selves.
   B) open, blind, hidden, and imagined selves.
   C) open, unopened, known, and unknown selves.
   D) moral, immoral, good, and bad selves.

   Answer: A
   Diff: 2   Page Ref: 75-77
   Skill: Factual

2) In regard to the blind area, we may correctly say which of the following?
   A) Communication does not improve as the blind area becomes smaller.
   B) People should be forced to see themselves as we see them.
   C) We control how much of the blind area we wish others to see of us.
   D) Communication is hindered by the very existence of the blind areas.

   Answer: D
   Diff: 2   Page Ref: 75-77
   Skill: Interpretive

3) Keeping the hidden area large involves
   A) an active process of keeping secrets.
   B) a passive process of keeping secrets.
   C) an active process of revealing secrets.
   D) a passive process of revealing secrets.

   Answer: A
   Diff: 2   Page Ref: 75-77
   Skill: Factual

4) We gain insight into the unknown self from which of the following?
   A) dreams
   B) hypnosis
   C) projective tests
   D) all of the above
   E) only A & C above

   Answer: D
   Diff: 2   Page Ref: 75-77
   Skill: Factual

5) The author offers the following suggestion for increasing self-awareness.

   A) conducting a dialogue with yourself

   B) increasing blind self

   C) avoiding your different selves

   D) decreasing your open self

   Answer: A
   Diff: 2   *Page Ref: 77*
   Skill: Factual

6) Among the advantages or virtues claimed for self-disclosure, the one that is NOT generally supported is:

   A) self-disclosure allows us to see through the rationalizations that we have built up.

   B) self-disclosure encourages self-acceptance.

   C) self-disclosure enables us to gain greater insight into our selves.

   D) self-disclosure can increase intrapersonal guilt.

   Answer: D
   Diff: 2   *Page Ref: 83–87*
   Skill: Interpretive

7) Self-disclosure refers to all of the following EXCEPT

   A) a type of communication.

   B) shared information.

   C) an interaction with at least one other person.

   D) an intrapersonal process.

   Answer: D
   Diff: 1   *Page Ref: 83–87*
   Skill: Factual

8) We may self-disclose in all of the following ways EXCEPT

   A) calling someone on the telephone.

   B) writing in a private diary.

   C) discussing in a large group.

   D) giving a public speech.

   Answer: B
   Diff: 1   *Page Ref: 83–87*
   Skill: Applied

9) Self-disclosure may
    A) be intrapersonal communication.
    B) involve information already known by others.
    C) be about feelings as well as behaviors.
    D) concern information about unrelated others.

    Answer: C
    Diff: 1   Page Ref: 83-87
    Skill: Factual

10) The main reason that both men and women give for avoiding self-disclosure is
    A) projecting an unfavorable image.
    B) giving information that will make them appear inconsistent.
    C) losing control over the other person.
    D) damaging relationships with people other than close acquaintances.

    Answer: A
    Diff: 2   Page Ref: 83-87
    Skill: Interpretive

11) In the corporate world, self-disclosures of alcoholism or drug-addiction are often followed by demotion, transfer, or dismissal. This danger of self-disclosure is known as:
    A) personal repition.
    B) material loss.
    C) social rejection.
    D) intrapersonal difficulties.

    Answer: B
    Diff: 2   Page Ref: 84
    Skill: Factual

12) When the mass media reveal a person's affectional orientation, it is known as:
    A) dating.
    B) dyadic effect.
    C) outing.
    D) communication efficiency.

    Answer: C
    Diff: 1   Page Ref: 85
    Skill: Interpretive

TRUE/FALSE. Write 'T' if the statement is true and 'F' if the statement is false.

1) The information known to both the self and to others is in the open self.

Answer: TRUE
Diff: 2   Page Ref: 75–77
Skill: Factual

2) As the size of the open self becomes larger, one or more of the other selves must get smaller.

Answer: TRUE
Diff: 2   Page Ref: 75–77
Skill: Interpretive

3) According to many communication theorists, such as Joseph Luft, the most effective communication occurs when there is a small open self so that a great deal of interest is maintained.

Answer: FALSE
Diff: 2   Page Ref: 75–77
Skill: Interpretive

4) Information that you know about yourself but that you do not share with others is in the blind area.

Answer: FALSE
Diff: 2   Page Ref: 75–77
Skill: Factual

5) The hidden self contains all that information that others know about you but you do not know about yourself.

Answer: FALSE
Diff: 2   Page Ref: 75–77
Skill: Factual

6) No one should hesitate to disclose information about himself or herself regardless of the immediate audience.

Answer: FALSE
Diff: 2   Page Ref: 83–87
Skill: Interpretive

7) Overt statements pertaining to the self as well as slips of the tongue, unconscious nonverbal movements, written confessions, and public confessions may all be examples of self-disclosure.

Answer: TRUE
Diff: 2   Page Ref: 83–87
Skill: Factual

8) Self-disclosure may be intrapersonal.

Answer: FALSE
Diff: 2   Page Ref: 83–87
Skill: Interpretive

9) People from Great Britain, Germany, the USA, and Puerto Rico are all more apt to disclose personal information (hobbies, attitudes, opinions on religion and politics) than information on finances, sex, personality, and interpersonal relationships.

Answer: TRUE
Diff: 2   Page Ref: 83–87
Skill: Interpretive

10) Self-disclosure enables us to get to know ourselves better.

Answer: TRUE
Diff: 1   Page Ref: 83–87
Skill: Factual

11) Self-disclosure enables us to deal better with our problems, especially our guilt.

Answer: TRUE
Diff: 1   Page Ref: 83–87
Skill: Factual

12) Self-acceptance is difficult to achieve without some degree of self-disclosure.

Answer: TRUE
Diff: 1   Page Ref: 83–87
Skill: Factual

13) Contrary to what would be expected, men are higher self-disclosurers than women are.

Answer: FALSE
Diff: 2   Page Ref: 83–87
Skill: Factual

14) Generally, people become more inhibited about self-disclosing after another person has self-disclosed.

Answer: FALSE
Diff: 2   Page Ref: 83–87
Skill: Interpretive

15) Self-disclosure is more likely to occur in a group of five or six than with only one other person.

Answer: FALSE
Diff: 2   Page Ref: 83–87
Skill: Interpretive

16) Husbands and wives self-disclose to each other more than they do to any other person or group of persons.

Answer: TRUE
Diff: 1   Page Ref: 83–87
Skill: Factual

17) The major reason that self-esteem is so important is simply that success breeds success.

Answer: TRUE
Diff: 1   Page Ref: 77–79
Skill: Interpretive

18) You control your thoughts and behaviors largely to the extent that you understand yourself and are aware of who you are.

Answer: TRUE
Diff: 1   Page Ref: 75–77
Skill: Factual

CHAPTER 6   Culture

MULTIPLE CHOICE. Choose the one alternative that best completes the statement or answers the question.

1) Direct eye contact from a younger person to an older person is considered disrespectful in which culture?
   A) American
   B) Japanese
   C) Indonesian
   D) German
   Answer: C
   Diff: 1   Page Ref: 90–95
   Skill: Applied

2) The assumption that the characteristics of language influence our cognitive processes, and that people speaking widely different languages also differ in how they view and think about the world (since languages differ greatly in regard to their semantic and structural characteristics) is known as
   A) linguistic ethnocentricism.
   B) linguistic determinism.
   C) linguistic relativity.
   D) linguistic enculturation.
   Answer: C
   Diff: 2   Page Ref: 90–95
   Skill: Factual

3) In low power distance cultures, power is more evenly distributed among the citizens. Which is a low power distance culture?
   A) Mexico
   B) India
   C) Denmark
   D) Brazil
   Answer: C
   Diff: 2   Page Ref: 90–95
   Skill: Interpretive

4) The stages of culture shock in the order in which they occur are
   A) honeymoon, adjustment, recovery, and crisis.
   B) adjustment, crisis, recovery, and honeymoon.
   C) crisis, recovery, adjustment, and honeymoon.
   D) honeymoon, crisis, recovery, and adjustment.

   Answer: D
   Diff: 1   *Page Ref: 103–104*
   Skill: Factual

5) Culture shock refers to the reaction one experiences at being placed in a culture that is very different from one's own or from what one is used to. This reaction is primarily
   A) sociological.
   B) psychological.
   C) communicational.
   D) anthropological.

   Answer: B
   Diff: 2   *Page Ref: 103–104*
   Skill: Factual

6) The author advises that in intercultural communication you do all EXCEPT which of the following?
   A) Ignore the differences between yourself and the culturally different.
   B) Recognize and reduce your ethnocentrism.
   C) Recognize meaning differences in verbal and nonverbal messages.
   D) Be mindful rather than mindless.

   Answer: A
   Diff: 2   *Page Ref: 98–104*
   Skill: Factual

7) The period of culture shock during which our feelings of inadequacy subside and we acquire the skills necessary to function effectively (for example, we learn the language or the ways of the new culture) is referred to as the
   A) crisis stage.
   B) honeymoon stage.
   C) adjustment stage.
   D) recovery stage.

   Answer: D
   Diff: 2   *Page Ref: 103–104*
   Skill: Factual

8) When we communicate a sense of togetherness to counteract the obvious intercultural differences, we are most clearly using the principle of

    A) supportiveness.

    B) confidence.

    C) immediacy.

    D) other–orientation.

Answer: C
Diff: 2   *Page Ref: 98–103*
Skill: Factual

9) Communicating genuine involvement in an intercultural interaction describes which principle of effective conversation?

    A) openness

    B) empathy

    C) positiveness

    D) expressiveness

Answer: D
Diff: 1   *Page Ref: 98–103*
Skill: Applied

10) A process by which we learn the culture into which we are born is

    A) acculturation.

    B) enculturation.

    C) enthnocentrism.

    D) collectivism.

Answer: B
Diff: 2   *Page Ref: 90*
Skill: Factual

11) Which is characteristic of individualistic or low–context cultures?

    A) The group's goals are most important.

    B) Cooperation is emphasized.

    C) Information is made explicit.

    D) Indirectness is valued.

Answer: C
Diff: 3   *Page Ref: 92–95*
Skill: Factual

TRUE/FALSE. Write 'T' if the statement is true and 'F' if the statement is false.

1) The general idea that language influences thought and, ultimately, behavior was given its strongest expression by linguistic anthropologists.

Answer: TRUE
Diff: 1   Page Ref: 93
Skill: Factual

2) The fact that Eskimos have numerous words for snow whereas in English there is but one, means that Eskimos have the ability to see kinds of snow that speakers of English cannot.

Answer: FALSE
Diff: 1   Page Ref: 93
Skill: Interpretive

3) When we ignore differences among the culturally different we are guilty of stereotyping.

Answer: TRUE
Diff: 2   Page Ref: 90–91
Skill: Factual

4) There is currently no evidence to support the notion that linguistic differences (whether semantic or structural) can influence behavior.

Answer: FALSE
Diff: 2   Page Ref: 100–101
Skill: Interpretive

5) The author advises that in attempting intercultural communication we should ignore the differences that exist within any one group.

Answer: FALSE
Diff: 2   Page Ref: 90–92
Skill: Factual

6) The most prevalent barrier to effective intercultural communication occurs when you assume that similarities exist and that differences do not.

Answer: TRUE
Diff: 2   Page Ref: 90–92
Skill: Factual

7) A high–context culture is a collectivist culture.

Answer: TRUE
Diff: 1   Page Ref: 92–94
Skill: Factual

8) Norway is a highly "feminine" culture in which both men and women are encouraged to be modest, oriented to maintaining the quality of life, and tender.

Answer: TRUE
Diff: 2   *Page Ref: 96–97*
Skill: Factual

CHAPTER 7   Verbal Messages

MULTIPLE CHOICE. Choose the one alternative that best completes the statement or answers the question.

1) Denotative meaning as compared with connotative meaning is

A) relatively unchanging.

B) more varied.

C) more emotional.

D) less useful.

Answer: A
Diff: 2   Page Ref: 108–110
Skill: Factual

2) Which is NOT an implication of the process view of meaning?

A) Meanings are in people not in words.

B) Meanings change constantly though words remain static.

C) Words may be culturally transmitted.

D) Words communicate only a small part of a person's total meaning.

Answer: C
Diff: 2   Page Ref: 108–111
Skill: Applied

3) Which statement is an example of an indirect statement?

A) I really like your new shirt.

B) No thanks. I'm really full.

C) Sorry, I am on a diet and can not eay anything with sugar.

D) I am really hungry for a hamburger tonight. How about you?

Answer: B
Diff: 2   Page Ref: 110–111
Skill: Applied

4) Direct messages usually accomplish all of the following EXCEPT

A) open responses.

B) honest responses.

C) resentful responses.

D) supportive responses.

Answer: C
Diff: 2   Page Ref: 110–111
Skill: Factual

5) The major difference between direct and indirect requests is
   A) direct requests are honest and open.
   B) indirect requests are honest and open.
   C) direct requests are often dishonest and manipulative.
   D) win–win outcomes are difficult to see with direct requests.

   Answer: A
   Diff: 2   *Page Ref: 110–111*
   Skill: Factual

6) This maxim or general communication principle molds that communication must be truthful.
   A) maxim of politeness
   B) maxim of quality
   C) maxim of relevance
   D) maxim of dominance

   Answer: B
   Diff: 2   *Page Ref: 109–110*
   Skill: Factual

7) In this maxim or general communication principle, if you're talking about A, B, and C and someone brings up D, you would assume that there's a connection between A, B, and C on the one hand and D on the other hand.
   A) maxim of politeness
   B) maxim of quality
   C) maxim of relevance
   D) maxim of quantity

   Answer: C
   Diff: 2   *Page Ref: 109–110*
   Skill: Factual

8) Disconfirmation is a communication pattern in which
   A) the speaker is very negative about his/her own message.
   B) you acknowledge the presence of someone and accept this person.
   C) interpersonal conflict is displaced through verbal expression.
   D) you ignore someone's presence as well as that person's communication.

   Answer: D
   Diff: 2   *Page Ref: 113*
   Skill: Factual

9) The rules for communicating politely over the Internet are known as the rules of

   A) context.

   B) bypassing.

   C) meaningfulness.

   D) netiquette.

Answer: D
Diff: 2   *Page Ref: 110*
Skill: Factual

10) Which is a disadvantage of indirect messages?

   A) They allow you to express a desire without offending anyone.

   B) They allow you to ask for compliments in a socially acceptable manner.

   C) They provide for you to be seen as manipulative.

   D) They provide for you to observe the rules of polite interaction.

Answer: C
Diff: 2   *Page Ref: 110-111*
Skill: Factual

11) Intensional orientation is seen when we

   A) divide the world into two classes.

   B) give primary attention to labels.

   C) confuse factual with inferential statements.

   D) fail to discriminate among and thereby discriminate against.

Answer: B
Diff: 2   *Page Ref: 119*
Skill: Factual

12) The correction for intensional orientation as a verbal communication barrier is to use an extensional orientation which can be described as

   A) the tendency to view people from their outside appearance.

   B) the tendency to view people in the way they are labeled by others.

   C) the tendency to look first to the actual people and only afterwards to their labels.

   D) the tendency to look first at other people's friends to help understand them.

Answer: C
Diff: 2   *Page Ref: 119*
Skill: Interpretive

13) Factual statements are characterized by all of the following EXCEPT that they
   A) are limited to what has been observed.
   B) may be made only by the observer.
   C) may be about any time--past, present, or future.

   Answer: C
   Diff: 2   Page Ref: 119-121
   Skill: Factual

14) Disraeli's advice, "To be conscious that you are ignorant is a great step toward knowledge," is appropriate advice for most persons, but relates most closely to those who are prone to
   A) intensional orientation.
   B) allness.
   C) fact-inference confusion.
   D) indiscrimination.

   Answer: B
   Diff: 3   Page Ref: 119
   Skill: Applied

15) When we focus on classes of individuals, objects or events and fail to see that each is unique, we are in the pattern of misevaluation called
   A) static evaluation.
   B) polarization.
   C) indiscrimination.
   D) fact-inference confusion.

   Answer: C
   Diff: 2   Page Ref: 119-124
   Skill: Factual

16) T.S. Eliot's observation that "what we know of other people is only our memory of the moments during which we knew them. And they have changed since then...at every meeting we are meeting a stranger" is a good warning against
   A) indiscrimination.
   B) static evaluation.
   C) fact-inference confusion.
   D) intensional orientation.

   Answer: B
   Diff: 3   Page Ref: 119-124
   Skill: Applied

17) When two people use the same word but mean different things and assume that since they used the same word they must, therefore, have the same meanings, this is the misevaluation known as

A) fact–inference confusion.

B) allness.

C) bypassing.

D) static evaluation.

Answer: C
Diff: 3   *Page Ref: 108–109*
Skill: Interpretive

18) The techniques of active listening--especially paraphrasing the speaker--are especially recommended as correctives for the misevaluation of

A) fact–inference confusion.

B) bypassing.

C) static evaluation.

D) indiscrimination.

Answer: B
Diff: 2   *Page Ref: 108–109*
Skill: Interpretive

19) The etc. is especially useful as a corrective for

A) fact–inference confusion.

B) allness.

C) bypassing.

D) indiscrimination.

Answer: B
Diff: 2   *Page Ref: 119–124*
Skill: Factual

20) The index is especially useful as a corrective for

A) fact–inference confusion.

B) allness.

C) indiscrimination.

D) bypassing.

Answer: C
Diff: 2   *Page Ref: 119–124*
Skill: Factual

21) The date is especially useful as a corrective for
   A) fact–inference confusion.
   B) allness.
   C) static evaluation.
   D) bypassing.

   Answer: C
   Diff: 2   *Page Ref: 119–124*
   Skill: Factual

22) Extensional orientation refers to
   A) the tendency to respond to labels as if they were the things which they represent.
   B) the tendency to respond to things as they are rather than as they are labeled or talked about.
   C) the tendency to see the middle ground as well as the extremes.
   D) the tendency to group unlike things together and to assume that because they have the same label, they are all alike.

   Answer: B
   Diff: 2   *Page Ref: 119–124*
   Skill: Factual

23) According to your author, which is true about word choice?
   A) "Lady is preferred to "woman" or "young woman."
   B) "Gay" is the preferred term for a woman who has an affectional preference for another woman.
   C) "Inuk" is preferred to "Eskimo."
   D) "Orientals" is a term preferred to "Asians."

   Answer: C
   Diff: 3   *Page Ref: 114–116*
   Skill: Factual

24) Factual statements have all of the following characteristics EXCEPT that they
   A) are limited to what has been observed.
   B) are loaded with evaluations.
   C) are subject to verifiable standards.
   D) may only be about the past or the present.

   Answer: D
   Diff: 2   *Page Ref: 119–120*
   Skill: Factual

25) Which does your author suggest for avoiding heterosexism?

A) Compliment gay men and lesbians because "they don't look it."
B) Assume that every gay man or lesbian knows what every other gay man or lesbian is thinking.
C) Say things like, "Lesbians are so loyal" or "Gay men are so open with their feelings."
D) Avoid over-attribution or the tendency to attribute just about everything a person does, says, and believes to being a gay man or lesbian.

Answer: D
Diff: 3   Page Ref: 115–116
Skill: Factual

26) Most lies are told to benefit the liar, generally, in order to do all EXCEPT

A) to increase desirable relationships.
B) to protect another's self-esteem.
C) to obtain money.
D) avoid punishment.

Answer: B
Diff: 3   Page Ref: 124–125
Skill: Factual

27) In an analysis of 322 lies, researchers found that

A) 75.8 percent benefited the liar.
B) 21.7 percent benefited some third party.
C) 2.5 percent benefited the person who was told the lie.
D) 42.7 percent benefited the liar's reference group.

Answer: A
Diff: 3   Page Ref: 124–125
Skill: Factual

28) Gossip is unethical in all of these instances EXCEPT

A) when we reveal information we promised to keep secret.
B) when it invades the privacy that everyone has a right to.
C) when it is nown to be false yet is passed on to others.
D) when the information will benefit relevant parties.

Answer: D
Diff: 3   Page Ref: 125
Skill: Factual

TRUE/FALSE. Write 'T' if the statement is true and 'F' if the statement is false.

1) Meanings are in people, not in words.

Answer: TRUE
Diff: 1   *Page Ref: 108*
Skill: Factual

2) The context of a communication situation has no impact on the meaning of the message.

Answer: FALSE
Diff: 1   *Page Ref: 109*
Skill: Factual

3) Connotative meanings are consistent, precise and standard.

Answer: FALSE
Diff: 1   *Page Ref: 110*
Skill: Factual

4) Meanings are really no more than just the words and gestures.

Answer: FALSE
Diff: 1   *Page Ref: 109*
Skill: Factual

5) Indirect messages allow us to express a desire without insulting or offending anyone.

Answer: TRUE
Diff: 1   *Page Ref: 110–112*
Skill: Factual

6) Polarization refers to our tendency to give first priority to words and only secondary attention to the reality.

Answer: FALSE
Diff: 2   *Page Ref: 119–124*
Skill: Factual

7) The map is not the territory.

Answer: TRUE
Diff: 1   *Page Ref: 119–124*
Skill: Factual

8) Factual and inferential statements can be distinguished from each other on the basis of their grammatical structure.

Answer: FALSE
Diff: 2   *Page Ref: 119–121*
Skill: Interpretive

9) Stereotyping is a form of indiscrimination.

Answer: TRUE
Diff: 2   *Page Ref: 114*
Skill: Interpretive

10) While there is nothing wrong with making inferential statements, the problem arises when we act as if those inferential statements are factual.

Answer: TRUE
Diff: 2   *Page Ref: 119–120*
Skill: Interpretive

11) While factual statements involve varying degrees of probability, inferential statements approach certainty.

Answer: FALSE
Diff: 2   *Page Ref: 119–120*
Skill: Interpretive

12) Lying may also be committed by omission as well as commission.

Answer: TRUE
Diff: 2   *Page Ref: 124–125*
Skill: Factual

13) Although most lies are verbal, some are nonverbal and most seem to involve at least some nonverbal elements.

Answer: TRUE
Diff: 2   *Page Ref: 124–125*
Skill: Factual

14) Most lies are told for two main reasons: 1) to gain some reward or 2) to avoid some punishment.

Answer: TRUE
Diff: 2   *Page Ref: 124–125*
Skill: Factual

15) Lies are often betrayed nonverbally.

Answer: TRUE
Diff: 1   *Page Ref: 124–125*
Skill: Factual

16) Gossip is an inevitable part of daily communication.

Answer: TRUE
Diff: 1   *Page Ref: 125*
Skill: Factual

17) According to your text, disconfirmation is the same as rejection.

Answer: FALSE
Diff: 1   *Page Ref: 113–114*
Skill: Factual

18) Heterosexist language is used to disparage gay men and lesbians.

Answer: TRUE
Diff: 1   *Page Ref: 115–116*
Skill: Factual

CHAPTER 8   Nonverbal Messages

MULTIPLE CHOICE. Choose the one alternative that best completes the statement or answers the question.

1) Scratching an itch on our heads in public and therefore limiting our scratching to something that might appear socially acceptable would be an example of

    A) emblems.

    B) adaptors.

    C) illustrators.

    D) affect displays.

Answer: B
Diff: 2   *Page Ref: 130–131*
Skill: Applied

2) Which of the following is an example of an emblem?

    A) turning your head to hear someone better.

    B) removing lint from someone's jacket.

    C) walking away from the person speaking.

    D) using the thumb's up for "good job."

Answer: D
Diff: 2   *Page Ref: 130–131*
Skill: Applied

3) Which of the following is true?

    A) Affect displays are always independent of verbal messages.

    B) Affect displays are always conscious.

    C) Affect displays are often unconscious.

    D) Affect displays are always intentional.

Answer: D
Diff: 2   *Page Ref: 130–131*
Skill: Interpretive

4) When we are listening to someone speak, we are not passive; rather, we nod our heads, purse our lips, make various paralinguistic sounds, and so on. These are all examples of

    A) emblems.

    B) illustrators.

    C) regulators.

    D) adaptors.

Answer: C
Diff: 2   *Page Ref: 130–131*
Skill: Interpretive

5) This facial management technique replaces or substitutes the expression of one emotion for another.

    A) intensifying

    B) deintensifying

    C) neutralizing

    D) making

Answer: D
Diff: 2   Page Ref: 131–132
Skill: Interpretive

6) Eye movements may serve all of the following functions EXCEPT

    A) to inform another that the communication channel is open for him or her to speak.

    B) to signal the nature of the relationship between two persons.

    C) to seek feedback from another.

    D) to provide most denotative meanings.

Answer: D
Diff: 2   Page Ref: 132–134
Skill: Factual

7) All are true about pupil dilation EXCEPT

    A) dilated pupils are judged more attractive than constricted ones.

    B) our pupils dilate when we look at something we evaluate negatively.

    C) pupil size reveals our level of emotional arousal.

    D) our pupils dilate when we are interested in something.

Answer: B
Diff: 2   Page Ref: 132–134
Skill: Factual

8) Mark Knapp identifies four major functions of eye communication; which is NOT one of those functions?

    A) to seek feedback

    B) to identify the listener's nonverbal messages

    C) to inform others to speak

    D) to signal the nature of the relationship

    E) to compensate for increased physical distance

Answer: B
Diff: 5   Page Ref: 132–134
Skill: Factual

9) Civil inattention can be defined as

   A) not caring what other people think of you.

   B) avoiding eye contact or averting our glance to maintain others' privacy.

   C) intrusions into other people's business.

   D) not looking when we really want to.

   Answer: B
   Diff: 2   Page Ref: 133–134
   Skill: Factual

10) Holding up two fingers while saying, "For my first point," is an example of a blend of verbal and nonverbal messages called

   A) contradicting.

   B) regulating.

   C) substituting.

   D) accenting.

   Answer: A
   Diff: 2   Page Ref: 130–131
   Skill: Applied

11) An example of substituting in verbal and nonverbal blends of messages would be

   A) raising your eyebrows while saying "Wow!"

   B) stressing the verb in your statement.

   C) holding up two fingers in a "V" to mean "peace."

   D) yelling to express your anger.

   Answer: C
   Diff: 2   Page Ref: 130–131
   Skill: Applied

12) This explains what happens when you increase or decrease the distance between yourself and another person in an interpersonal interaction.

   A) haptics

   B) chronemics

   C) expectancy violations theory

   D) secondary territories

   Answer: C
   Diff: 3   Page Ref: 134–137
   Skill: Interpretive

13) Silence is used for all of the following purposes EXCEPT
   A) allowing the speaker time to think.
   B) as a weapon to hurt others.
   C) as a response to personal anxiety, shyness, or threats.
   D) to verbalize and detail a viewpoint.
   E) when you have nothing to say.

   Answer: D
   Diff: 2   Page Ref: 143–144
   Skill: Factual

14) Which of the following statements is true?
   A) Although Japanese people consider direct eye contact an expression of honesty, Americans see this as a lack of respect.
   B) Pointing with the index finger is seen as polite in many Middle–Eastern countries.
   C) In Thailand black signifies purity and white signifies old age.
   D) Qahr is more frequently initiated between two women than between two men, but it lasts longer between men and often requires a mediator to establish ashti.
   E) Germans and Scandinavians operate on polychronic time while Arabs and Latin Americans on monochronic time.

   Answer: D
   Diff: 3   Page Ref: 132–146
   Skill: Interpretive

15) The study of how people unconsciously structure our physical space is referred to as
   A) proxemics.
   B) kinesics.
   C) paralinguistics.
   D) disnetics.

   Answer: A
   Diff: 1   Page Ref: 134–135
   Skill: Factual

16) In his study of space, Edward T. Hall specified four major distances?
   A) physical, psychological, sociological, and anthropological
   B) hate, indifference, like, and love
   C) intimate, personal, social, and public
   D) proxemic, territorial, encroachment, and marking

   Answer: C
   Diff: 1   Page Ref: 134–137
   Skill: Factual

17) Which of the following is NOT supported by contemporary research?1
   A) People of equal status will generally maintain a closer distance between themselves than will people of unequal status.
   B) When the status between two persons is unequal, the lower-status person approaches the higher-status person more closely than the higher-status person approaches the lower-status person.
   C) A higher-status person may approach the territory of a lower-status person but not visa versa.
   D) Women generally stand closer to each other than men.

Answer: B
Diff: 3   *Page Ref: 135–138*
Skill: Interpretive

18) Which of the following is supported by contemporary research?
   A) Cultures that keep substantial distances between them also engage in extensive interpersonal touching.
   B) The larger the physical space we are in, the greater the interpersonal space we maintain between each other.
   C) In discussing personal matters, we maintain a closer physical distance than when we talk about impersonal, matters.
   D) People who are low in apprehension are generally high in touch avoidance.

Answer: C
Diff: 3   *Page Ref: 135*
Skill: Applied

19) Which of the following is NOT supported by contemporary research findings on the factors that influence our proxemic behavior?
   A) We stand farther apart from friends than from enemies.
   B) We stand farther apart from authority figures than from peers.
   C) We stand closer to those who are physically handicapped than from the nonhandicapped.
   D) We stand closer to those of a different racial group than from our own racial group.

Answer: B
Diff: 3   *Page Ref: 135–136*
Skill: Interpretive

20) The name plate on your instructor's door is an example of
   A) a central marker.
   B) a boundary marker.
   C) an ear marker.
   D) a linear marker.

Answer: C
Diff: 1   *Page Ref: 137*
Skill: Applied

21) The cushions on a couch that divide the seating areas are examples of
    A) central markers.
    B) boundary markers.
    C) ear markers.
    D) lineal markers.

Answer: B
Diff: 1   Page Ref: 137
Skill: Applied

22) Among the meanings of touch identified by Jones and Yarbrough are all of the following EXCEPT
    A) positive feelings.
    B) ritual and task-relatedness.
    C) play and control.
    D) encroachment and marking.

Answer: D
Diff: 2   Page Ref: 140-142
Skill: Factual

23) When someone helps someone else on a bus into a seat, the function of that touch is best described as
    A) positive affect.
    B) marking.
    C) task-relatedness.
    D) ritual.

Answer: C
Diff: 2   Page Ref: 140-142
Skill: Applied

24) Research on touch avoidance supports all EXCEPT which of the following?
    A) People who score high on touch avoidance also score high on communication apprehension.
    B) People who score high on touch avoidance also score high on self-disclosure.
    C) Men score higher on same-sex touch avoidance than do women.
    D) Women score higher on opposite-sex touch avoidance than do men.

Answer: B
Diff: 3   Page Ref: 140-142
Skill: Factual

25) The student who comes into a lecture hall early, places books and jacket on a seat, and goes out to talk with friends has engaged in behavior best described as

A) dominance marker.

B) transactional identifier.

C) relational connector.

D) territorial marker.

Answer: D
Diff: 1   Page Ref: 136–137
Skill: Applied

26) You see events as circular and recurring. The wisdom of yesterday is applicable also to today and tomorrow. This orientation to time is called

A) present.

B) past.

C) future.

D) progressive.

Answer: B
Diff: 2   Page Ref: 144–146
Skill: Applied

27) These people have a strong work ethic and are committed to completing a task despite difficulties and temptations. This time orientation is called a

A) perseverance orientation.

B) partying orientation.

C) worry-free orientation.

D) goal-seeking and planning orientation.

Answer: A
Diff: 2   Page Ref: 144–146
Skill: Applied

TRUE/FALSE. Write 'T' if the statement is true and 'F' if the statement is false.

1) Emblems are nonverbal behaviors that rather directly translate words or phrases.
Answer: TRUE
Diff: 2   Page Ref: 130–131
Skill: Factual

2) Illustrators are nonverbal behaviors that monitor, maintain, or control the speaking of another individual.
Answer: FALSE
Diff: 2   Page Ref: 130–131
Skill: Interpretive

3) Affect displays are the movements of the facial area that convey emotional meaning; these are the facial expressions that show anger and fear, happiness and surprise.

Answer: TRUE
Diff: 2   Page Ref: 148
Skill: Factual

4) Adaptors are nonverbal behaviors that accompany and illustrate the verbal messages.

Answer: FALSE
Diff: 2   Page Ref: 148
Skill: Interpretive

5) Speakers gaze at listeners more than listeners gaze at speakers.

Answer: FALSE
Diff: 2   Page Ref: 132–134
Skill: Factual

6) The eight emotions identified by Ekman et al. are generally called primary affect displays.

Answer: TRUE
Diff: 1   Page Ref: 130–131
Skill: Factual

7) Accuracy of encoding and decoding facial emotions is affected solely by age.

Answer: FALSE
Diff: 1   Page Ref: 131–132
Skill: Interpretive

8) There is at least some indication that we do communicate emotions without being aware of it or even without observers being aware of it.

Answer: TRUE
Diff: 1   Page Ref: 131–132
Skill: Interpretive

9) The messages communicated by the eyes vary depending on the duration, direction, and quality of the eye behavior.

Answer: TRUE
Diff: 2   Page Ref: 132–134
Skill: Applied

10) A great deal more touching is reported among opposite-sex friends than among same-sex friends.

Answer: TRUE
Diff: 1   Page Ref: 140–142
Skill: Factual

11) The studies conducted on touching show that touching behavior is the same regardless of the culture.

Answer: FALSE
Diff: 1   Page Ref: 140–142
Skill: Factual

12) Spatial relationships are the same in all cultures for which we have records.

Answer: FALSE
Diff: 1   Page Ref: 134–136
Skill: Interpretive

13) The personal distance is the closest of Hall's four distances and ranges from the close phase of actual touching to the far phase of six to 18 inches.

Answer: FALSE
Diff: 2   Page Ref: 134–135
Skill: Factual

14) If enough space is not available to maintain a social distance, then it is possible to arrange space so that a social distance is created psychologically if not physically.

Answer: TRUE
Diff: 2   Page Ref: 136–137
Skill: Interpretive

15) The more future oriented a person is, the greater that person's income is likely to be.

Answer: TRUE
Diff: 3   Page Ref: 144–146
Skill: Factual

CHAPTER 9   Interpersonal Communication: Conversation

MULTIPLE CHOICE. Choose the one alternative that best completes the statement or answers the question.

1) Which of the following propositions or assumptions concerning the five–stage model of conversation is NOT true?

   A) We may exit from any stage in the relationship.

   B) We may go back to a less intense relationship or forward to a more intense relationship.

   C) We go from one stage to another without ever skipping a stage.

   D) We may spend different amounts of time at each stage, i.e., there is no specified time which must be spent at one stage before moving to a more intense stage.

Answer: C
Diff: 2   Page Ref: 153–154
Skill: Factual

2) Conversation rule violations include all of the following EXCEPT

   A) using openings that are sensitive.

   B) omitting feedforward before a truly shocking message.

   C) doing business without the normally expected greeting.

   D) omitting an appropriate closing.

Answer: A
Diff: 3   Page Ref: 156–157
Skill: Factual

3) Langer offers this suggestion to increase mindfulness in conversation:

   A) Rely heavily on first impressions.

   B) Be open to new information unless it contradicts your firmly held stereotypes.

   C) See your own and other's behaviors from a variety of perspectives.

   D) Store an image of a person under one specific label only.

Answer: C
Diff: 3   Page Ref: 159
Skill: Applied

4) This skill of conversational competence communicates genuine involvement in the interpersonal interaction.

   A) openness

   B) empathy

   C) immediacy

   D) expressiveness

   E) other–orientation

   Answer: D

   Diff: 2   Page Ref: 163–166

   Skill: Factual

5) This skill of conversational competence refers to the joining of the speaker and listener, the creation of a sense of togetherness.

   A) openness

   B) empathy

   C) positiveness

   D) immediacy

   E) interaction management

   Answer: D

   Diff: 2   Page Ref: 163–166

   Skill: Factual

6) Asking if it's all right to dump your troubles on someone before doing so or asking if your phone call comes at an in opportune time before launching into your conversation demonstrates

   A) self–orientation.

   B) hedging.

   C) other–orientation.

   D) credentialing.

   Answer: C

   Diff: 3   Page Ref: 169–170

   Skill: Applied

7) "Could you show me how to work this machine?" is an example of which of the lines for opening conversation?

   A) cute–flippant opener

   B) innocuous opener

   C) direct opener

   D) opener

   Answer: B

   Diff: 2   Page Ref: 156

   Skill: Applied

8) Avoiding eye contact with the listener so there is no indication that the speaker is passing the speaking turn on to the listener is an example of

 A) turn–yielding.

 B) back–channeling.

 C) turn–denying.

 D) turn–maintaining.

 Answer: D
 Diff: 2   Page Ref: 159
 Skill: Factual

9) DeFrancisco (1991) discovered that in married couples

 A) men silence women.

 B) most violations of turn–taking are committed by men.

 C) the most common violation of turn–taking is no response.

 D) all of the above

 E) none of the above

 Answer: D
 Diff: 3   Page Ref: 156–159
 Skill: Factual

10) "Right," "Exactly," and "Of course" are examples of

 A) back–channeling.

 B) turn–requesting.

 C) interruptions.

 D) phatic communication.

 Answer: A
 Diff: 2   Page Ref: 156–159
 Skill: Applied

11) "I know you'll think this suggestion is out of order, but please consider" is an example of

 A) a cognitive disclaimer.

 B) a sin license.

 C) credentialing.

 D) an appeal for the suspension of judgment.

 Answer: B
 Diff: 3   Page Ref: 170
 Skill: Applied

12) "If you promise not to laugh, I'll tell you exactly what happened" is an example of

    A) a cognitive disclaimer.

    B) hedging.

    C) an appeal for the suspension of judgment.

    D) a sin license.

    Answer: C
    Diff: 3   *Page Ref: 170*
    Skill: Applied

13) Which is NOT one of the three types of excuses?

    A) Yes, but type

    B) I didn't do it type

    C) Worry type

    D) It wasn't so bad type

    Answer: A
    Diff: 3   *Page Ref: 170–172*
    Skill: Factual

14) "I know this may not be the place to discuss business, but ..." is an example of which conversational disclaimer?

    A) hedging

    B) credentialing

    C) sin licensing

    D) cognitive disclaimer

    E) appeal for the suspension of judgment

    Answer: C
    Diff: 2   *Page Ref: 172*
    Skill: Factual

15) "Don't get the wrong idea; I'm not sexist, but..." is an example of which conversational disclaimer?

    A) hedging

    B) credentialing

    C) sin licensing

    D) cognitive disclaimer

    E) appeals for the suspension of judgment

    Answer: B
    Diff: 2   *Page Ref: 170*
    Skill: Applied

16) Cognitive disclaimers can be described as when the speaker

   A) disclaims the importance of the message to his/her own identity.
   B) knows that the message may be poorly received, but will say it anyway.
   C) announces that he/she will commit a violation of some social or cultural rule but should be "forgiven" in advance.
   D) asks the listener to delay making judgment.
   E) seeks to reaffirm his/her cognitive abilities in anticipation of the listeners doubting him/her.

Answer: E
Diff: 3   Page Ref: 170
Skill: Factual

TRUE/FALSE. Write 'T' if the statement is true and 'F' if the statement is false.

1) Feedforward is the substance or focus of a conversation.

Answer: FALSE
Diff: 2   Page Ref: 153–154
Skill: Factual

2) Kim tells us that effectiveness in intercultural settings requires us to be tolerant of other attitudes, values, and ways of doing things.

Answer: TRUE
Diff: 2   Page Ref: 162–163
Skill: Interpretive

3) The overly expressive listener waits for a cue to take over the speaking turn.

Answer: FALSE
Diff: 2   Page Ref: 167–168
Skill: Factual

4) High self-monitors are not concerned with the image they present to others.

Answer: FALSE
Diff: 2   Page Ref: 166–167
Skill: Interpretive

5) The process of conversation takes place in at least eight steps.

Answer: FALSE
Diff: 2   Page Ref: 153
Skill: Applied

6) The basis of effective conversation is understanding through an agreed upon cooperation between speaker and listener.

Answer: TRUE
Diff: 2   *Page Ref: 153–155*
Skill: Applied

7) Turn-maintaining cues tell the listener that the speaker is finished and wishes to exchange the role of speaker for that of listener.

Answer: FALSE
Diff: 2   *Page Ref: 156–157*
Skill: Factual

8) Back-channeling cues are used to communicate various types of information back to the speaker without assuming the role of the speaker.

Answer: TRUE
Diff: 2   *Page Ref: 156–157*
Skill: Factual

9) As a listener, you can regulate the conversation by using three types of cues such as turn-maintaining and turn-yielding cues.

Answer: FALSE
Diff: 2   *Page Ref: 156–157*
Skill: Applied

10) Sin licenses help you establish your special qualifications for saying what you are about to say.

Answer: FALSE
Diff: 2   *Page Ref: 170*
Skill: Factual

11) A disclaimer helps you to separate yourself from the message so that if your listeners reject your message, they need not reject you.

Answer: FALSE
Diff: 1   *Page Ref: 170*
Skill: Factual

12) The excuse, ideally, lessens the negative impact of the message.

Answer: TRUE
Diff: 2   *Page Ref: 170–173*
Skill: Factual

13) Excuses pervade all forms of communication.

Answer: TRUE
Diff: 1　　*Page Ref: 170–173*
Skill: Factual

14) The best excuses are apologies.

Answer: TRUE
Diff: 1　　*Page Ref: 170–173*
Skill: Factual

15) The least preferred opening lines by both men and women are generally those that are direct or innocuous.

Answer: FALSE
Diff: 2　　*Page Ref: 156*
Skill: Factual

16) The most preferred lines by both men and women are those that are cute-flippant.

Answer: FALSE
Diff: 2　　*Page Ref: 156*
Skill: Factual

17) According to the spiral of silence theory, when you feel your opinions are in agreement with the majority, you are more likely to voice them than if you feel they are in disagreement.

Answer: TRUE
Diff: 3　　*Page Ref: 168*
Skill: Interpretive

ESSAY. Write your answer in the space provided or on a separate sheet of paper.

1) Identify some motives for excuse-making and three specific types of excuses according to the text.

Answer: Students should be able to provide examples of excuse-making motives and the three specific types of excuses.
Diff: 2　　*Page Ref: 170–172*
Skill: Applied

2) Explain the five-step conversational process by selecting key examples of dialogue from your conversations.

Answer: Students should be able to identify the five steps of the conversational process. Examples of dialogue should clearly illustrate the five steps.
Diff: 3　　*Page Ref: 153–155*
Skill: Applied

3) Select one of the five disclaimers used in preventing conversational problems and provide an example of how you have used this disclaimer in conversation.

Answer: Students may select one of the five disclaimers identified.

Diff: 3   Page Ref: 170

Skill: Applied

CHAPTER 10   Interpersonal Relationship

MULTIPLE CHOICE. Choose the one alternative that best completes the statement or answers the question.

1) All of the following are methods of making verbal contact after the initial nonverbal communication EXCEPT
   A) focus the conversation on yourself so the other person can get to know you.
   B) focus the conversation on the other person.
   C) exchange favors and rewards.
   D) establish commonalities.

   Answer: A
   Diff: 2   Page Ref: 175-176
   Skill: Applied

2) Among the reasons for relationship development are all of the following EXCEPT
   A) to lessen loneliness.
   B) to secure stimulation.
   C) to acquire self–knowledge.
   D) to minimize pleasures, to maximize pains.

   Answer: D
   Diff: 2   Page Ref: 175–176
   Skill: Factual

3) Qualifiers refer to
   A) the attitudes of an individual that are similar to or different from our own.
   B) the availability of an individual for a relationship.
   C) the qualities that make the individual you wish to encounter an appropriate choice.
   D) the phatic messages that we send in our initial interaction.

   Answer: C
   Diff: 2   Page Ref: 177
   Skill: Factual

4) Which of the following propositions is true?
   A) The man often becomes resentful if the woman fulfills his expectations concerning household duties.
   B) Although sexual frequency is not related to relational breakdown, sexual satisfaction is.
   C) Men who are ambitious in work are less appreciated by their partners.
   D) Relationships with ambitious women are more stable than those with unambitious women.

   Answer: B
   Diff: 3   *Page Ref: 178–179*
   Skill: Factual

5) Which of the following propositions concerning sex and relational development and deterioration is false?
   A) Sexual problems frequently rank among the top three in studies of newlyweds.
   B) Sexual frequency is related to relational breakdown.
   C) Open relationships are less stable than the traditional closed relationships.
   D) Extrarelational affairs contribute significantly to breakups for all types of couples.

   Answer: B
   Diff: 3   *Page Ref: 177–178*
   Skill: Factual

6) Which is NOT a stage in the six major stages of interpersonal relationships?
   A) contact and involvement
   B) intimacy and deterioration
   C) progress and regress
   D) repair and dissolution

   Answer: C
   Diff: 2   *Page Ref: 176*
   Skill: Factual

7) There are dynamic tensions within each relationship stage. This dynamic tension relates to the desires to be in an exclusive relationship and one that is open to different people.
   A) autonomy and connection
   B) novelty and predictability
   C) closedness and openness
   D) deterioration and repair

   Answer: A
   Diff: 3   *Page Ref: 175*
   Skill: Applied

8) Of the following communication patterns that seem to characterize relational deterioration, which is true?

   A) a decrease

   B) an increase in self-disclosure

   C) an increase in negative evaluation and a decrease in positive evaluation

   D) an increase in requests for pleasurable behaviors and a decrease in requests to stop unpleasant or negative behaviors

   Answer: C
   Diff: 3   Page Ref: 178–180
   Skill: Factual

9) Thinking that you will want to spend all of your time together in a relationship is an example of which cause of relationship deterioration?

   A) relational changes

   B) sex

   C) unrealistic expectations

   D) work

   E) financial difficulties

   Answer: C
   Diff: 2   Page Ref: 178–180
   Skill: Interpretive

10) Which one of the following statements is NOT one of the six strategies recommended by the author for relationship repair?

   A) Affirm each other.

   B) Take risks.

   C) Engage in productive conflict resolution.

   D) Avoid confrontations at all costs.

   Answer: D
   Diff: 2   Page Ref: 183–185
   Skill: Factual

11) Using lies to avoid arguments over changed behavior patterns is an example of which communication pattern change exhibited during relationship deterioration?

   A) withdrawal

   B) deception

   C) self-disclosure

   D) favor exchange

   Answer: B
   Diff: 2   Page Ref: 183–185
   Skill: Interpretive

12) Which is a valid reason for developing relationships?

    A) to increase loneliness

    B) to secure stimulation

    C) to minimize pleasure

    D) to maximize pain

Answer: B
Diff: 3   *Page Ref: 175–176*
Skill: Factual

13) Which of these statements about maintaining relationships is FALSE?

    A) Individuals have an emotional attachment to each other.

    B) Financial advantages motivate many couples to stay together.

    C) Fear motivates many couples to stay together.

    D) The absence of inertia keeps many couples together.

Answer: D
Diff: 3   *Page Ref: 181–183*
Skill: Factual

14) All relationships are held together, in part, by one or some combination of

    A) want, obligation, or necessity.

    B) frequency, intensity, or duration.

    C) inertia, fear, or children.

    D) convenience, emotional attachment, or money.

Answer: A
Diff: 3   *Page Ref: 181–183*
Skill: Factual

15) This maintenance strategy for relationships includes being polite, cheerful, friendly and avoiding criticism.

    A) togetherness behaviors

    B) ceremonial behaviors

    C) prosocial behaviors

    D) sharing joint activities

Answer: C
Diff: 3   *Page Ref: 181–183*
Skill: Factual

16) In this strategy of interpersonal repair, the couple specifies what is wrong with the relationship and what changes would be needed to make it better.

A) risk

B) affirm each other

C) recognize the problem

D) engage in productive conflict resolution

Answer: C

Diff: 3   *Page Ref: 183–185*

Skill: Factual

17) According to the text, reciprocity may be defined as friendship

A) based on imbalance.

B) characterized by helping to correct another's faults.

C) which involves a cordial but not intense relationship.

D) based on equality.

Answer: D

Diff: 3   *Page Ref: 197*

Skill: Factual

18) When you are attracted to others who are like you, which factor in attraction theory is active?

A) attractiveness

B) similarity

C) proximity

D) reinforcement

Answer: B

Diff: 3   *Page Ref: 197*

Skill: Factual

19) When you are attracted to others who give us rewards, which factor in attraction theory is active?

A) attractiveness

B) similarity

C) proximity

D) reinforcement

Answer: D

Diff: 3   *Page Ref: 197*

Skill: Factual

20) Which of the following describes a lover that is practical and seeks a relationship that will work?

    A) ludus

    B) pragma

    C) erotic

    D) agape

Answer: B
Diff: 2   *Page Ref: 187–188*
Skill: Factual

21) All of the following are characteristics of storage love EXCEPT

    A) peaceful and tranquil.

    B) lacks passion and intensity.

    C) plagued by sexual difficulties.

    D) a comparison–like relationship.

Answer: C
Diff: 2   *Page Ref: 187–188*
Skill: Applied

22) In their relationship, Kimberly and Alan eat their meals together, present themselves to others as a unified couple, and seldom if ever have sex–role conflicts. With regard to their relationship, they would be referred to as

    A) separates.

    B) independents.

    C) traditionals.

    D) parallelists.

Answer: C
Diff: 2   *Page Ref: 190*
Skill: Applied

23) Independents have this in common:

    A) they avoid conflict.

    B) each ritualizes time together.

    C) a feeling that other persons cannot be brought into the relationship.

    D) they are relatively androgynous.

Answer: D
Diff: 3   *Page Ref: 190*
Skill: Interpretive

24) "Separates" have this in common:

   A) to separates, the relationship is more love than convenience.

   B) separates experience greater sharing.

   C) view their relationship as being a matter of convenience.

   D) separates see themselves a part of a "we".

   Answer: C
   Diff: 3   Page Ref: 190
   Skill: Interpretive

25) When a relationship begins to deteriorate, the breadth and depth will, in many ways, reverse themselves. This process is called

   A) penetration.

   B) personalness.

   C) depenetration.

   D) maximization.

   Answer: C
   Diff: 3   Page Ref: 197
   Skill: Factual

26) In social exchange theory, this is a general idea of the kinds of rewards and profits that you feel you ought to get out of such a relationship.

   A) equity

   B) ratio

   C) comparison level

   D) romantic rules

   Answer: C
   Diff: 2   Page Ref: 197
   Skill: Factual

27) This theory claims that you develop and maintain relationships in which the RATIO of your rewards compared to costs is approximately equal to your partner's.

   A) Social exchange theory

   B) Equity theory

   C) Attraction theory

   D) Social penetration theory

   Answer: B
   Diff: 3   Page Ref: 197
   Skill: Factual

TRUE/FALSE. Write 'T' if the statement is true and 'F' if the statement is false.

1) Among the reasons why relationships develop is the desire or need to acquire self-knowledge.

   Answer: TRUE
   Diff: 2   *Page Ref: 175-176*
   Skill: Interpretive

2) In initiating relationships, we should determine clearance before examining the qualifiers. Conflict can be avoided in any meaningful relationship.

   Answer: FALSE
   Diff: 2   *Page Ref: 175-176*
   Skill: Factual

3) Sexual problems rank among the bottom three problems in almost all studies of newlyweds. Most people generally agree on what conflict is and how it operates.

   Answer: FALSE
   Diff: 1   *Page Ref: 179-180*
   Skill: Factual

4) Unlike sexual or work-related difficulties, financial difficulties generally do not influence or interact with other relationship dimensions to create further problems.

   Answer: FALSE
   Diff: 1   *Page Ref: 180*
   Skill: Factual

5) Few couples stay together for a single reason.

   Answer: TRUE
   Diff: 1   *Page Ref: 178-180*
   Skill: Factual

6) A relationship in which each person pays about the same costs but one person derives substantially greater reward will create problems for the relationship, according to the equity theory.

   Answer: TRUE
   Diff: 2   *Page Ref: 197*
   Skill: Factual

7) Generally, during relationship deterioration we engage in greater self-disclosure.

   Answer: FALSE
   Diff: 2   *Page Ref: 178-180*
   Skill: Factual

8) Human beings need stimulation and consequently seek relationships for mental and physical stimulation.

Answer: TRUE
Diff: 1   *Page Ref: 176–177*
Skill: Factual

9) For any relationship to improve, you must be willing to take risks. After the conflict is over, the best thing to do is to forget about it.

Answer: TRUE
Diff: 1   *Page Ref: 185–186*
Skill: Factual

10) A friendship of receptivity may be defined as an interpersonal relationship in which one person is the primary giver and one the primary receiver.

Answer: TRUE
Diff: 1   *Page Ref: 187*
Skill: Factual

11) You are attracted to people YOU reward.

Answer: TRUE
Diff: 2   *Page Ref: 190–191*
Skill: Factual

12) Generally, people attribute negative characteristics to people they find unattractive and positive characteristics to people they find attractive.

Answer: TRUE
Diff: 2   *Page Ref: 190–191*
Skill: Factual

13) You come to like people for whom YOU do favors.

Answer: TRUE
Diff: 2   *Page Ref: 190–191*
Skill: Factual

14) According to the relationship rules approach, friendship and love is held together by adherence to certain rules.

Answer: TRUE
Diff: 1   *Page Ref: 197*
Skill: Factual

15) In support of equity theory, research shows that the overbenefited person is often quite unhappy and discontented.

Answer: FALSE
Diff: 2   *Page Ref: 197*
Skill: Factual

16) The number of topics about which the individuals communicate is referred to as the integration of the interaction.

Answer: FALSE
Diff: 1   *Page Ref: 194*
Skill: Factual

17) Generally, physical attractiveness is an asset for women and a liability for men.

Answer: FALSE
Diff: 1   *Page Ref: 190–191*
Skill: Factual

18) In addition to liking those who reward us, we also increase our liking for those whom we reward.

Answer: TRUE
Diff: 1   *Page Ref: 190–191*
Skill: Factual

19) The matching hypothesis would predict that we would date and eventually mate with those who complement us.

Answer: FALSE
Diff: 1   *Page Ref: 195–196*
Skill: Factual

20) A parasocial relationship is one in which you see yourself as having a media personality.

Answer: TRUE
Diff: 1   *Page Ref: 191*
Skill: Factual

ESSAY. Write your answer in the space provided or on a separate sheet of paper.

1) List the three stages of friendship development. Provide a brief example of each.

Answer: Students would use data from the formula to explain the three stages. Additionally, they should provide examples of each. For example, initial contact and acquaintanceship -- when you introduce yourself to a classmate beside you at the start of a new school term.

Diff: 2   *Page Ref: 187*
Skill: Applied

2) Explain the concept of love.

Answer: Students should explain Davis' identification. Additionally, they should provide the brief specifics of each.

Diff: 2   Page Ref: 255

Skill: Applied

3) List and explain the six types of love.

Answer: Students should list and explain the six types of love.

Diff: 3   Page Ref: 187–188

Skill: Applied

4) List and explain the relationship theories and movements.

Answer: Students should use the information in table 10.2 to develop their response fully.

Diff: 2   Page Ref: 197

Skill: Factual

CHAPTER 11   Interpersonal Conflict

MULTIPLE CHOICE. Choose the one alternative that best completes the statement or answers the question.

1) Different cultures view conflict management techniques differently. Which is true?
   A) White females were found to use more direct controlling strategies than did African American females.
   B) African American and white men tended to avoid or withdraw from relationship conflict.
   C) Anglo American men preferred flexibility while women preferred direct and rational argument.
   D) African American women emphasized mutual understanding achieved through discussing the reasons for the conflict while Mexican American men focused on support for the relationship.

   Answer: B
   Diff: 3   Page Ref: 203–204
   Skill: Interpretive

2) In this online conflict, one user sends messages that personally attack another user.
   A) spamming
   B) posting
   C) flaming
   D) locking and loading

   Answer: C
   Diff: 2   Page Ref: 205–206
   Skill: Factual

3) Which of these is true?
   A) In Quebec, a couple's "first big fight" is over jealousy.
   B) Students from collective cultures preferred a conflict style that was adversarial and confrontational.
   C) Students from individualistic cultures preferred a conflict style of mediation and bargaining.
   D) Asian cultures are more strongly prohibitive of women's conflict strategies.

   Answer: D
   Diff: 3   Page Ref: 203–204
   Skill: Interpretive

4) When Pat does not get exactly what Pat wants, Pat cries until Chris agrees to whatever they have been arguing about. We would classify Pat's conflict strategy as

    A) gunnysacking.

    B) personal rejection.

    C) silencing.

    D) force.

Answer: C
Diff: 2   *Page Ref: 210*
Skill: Applied

5) A relational conflict would center on

    A) the value of a particular movie.

    B) how to spend your savings.

    C) intrapersonal cognitive dissonance.

    D) who is in charge.

Answer: D
Diff: 3   *Page Ref: 201*
Skill: Factual

6) Content conflict centers on

    A) the content of the relationship between the two individuals involved.

    B) the equality of the primary relationship.

    C) objects, events, and persons external (usually) to the relationship.

    D) rights to set down rules of behaviors.

Answer: C
Diff: 3   *Page Ref: 201*
Skill: Factual

7) A person who stores up grievances against another person and unloads these during a conflict situation is engaging in the unproductive strategy known as

    A) glitterdoming.

    B) gunnysacking.

    C) silencing.

    D) stonewalling.

Answer: B
Diff: 2   *Page Ref: 210*
Skill: Factual

8) When Pat and Chris argue, Pat's all-too-frequent strategy is to bring up all of Chris's previous failures and indiscretions. Pat's behavior is best described as

A) redefinition.

B) minimization.

C) gunnysacking.

D) beltlining.

Answer: C
Diff: 2   *Page Ref: 210*
Skill: Applied

9) A negative aspect of conflict does this:

A) increases negative regard for the opponent.

B) increases energy.

C) stops resentment from increasing.

D) enables you to state what you each want and perhaps get it.

Answer: A
Diff: 3   *Page Ref: 204*
Skill: Factual

10) A positive aspect of conflict does this:

A) prevents hostilities and resentments from festering.

B) increases costs.

C) decreases rewards.

D) closes us off from the other person.

Answer: A
Diff: 3   *Page Ref: 204-205*
Skill: Factual

11) Nonnegotiation can best be described as

A) a special type of avoidance in conflict called "steamrolling."

B) trying to listen to the other person's argument.

C) not expressing your own point of view in an argument.

D) trying to discuss the conflict but not getting anywhere.

Answer: A
Diff: 2   *Page Ref: 207*
Skill: Interpretive

12) Verbal aggressiveness can do all of the following EXCEPT

A) inflict psychological pain.

B) attack the other person's self-concept.

C) increase the effectiveness of the conflict management strategy.

D) disconfirm and discredit the individual's view of self.

Answer: C

Diff: 2   *Page Ref: 212-213*

Skill: Interpretive

13) Which of the following is NOT a suggestion to prevent argumentativeness from degenerating into verbal aggressiveness?

A) Treat disagreements as subjectively as possible.

B) Avoid attacking the other person.

C) Avoid presenting your arguments too emotionally.

D) Allow the other person to save face.

Answer: A

Diff: 3   *Page Ref: 212-213*

Skill: Applied

14) Before the conflict, all of the following statements are suggestions to help make the conflict productive EXCEPT

A) never fight in private.

B) be sure you are each ready to fight.

C) know what you're fighting about.

D) only fight about problems that can be solved.

Answer: A

Diff: 2   *Page Ref: 215-216*

Skill: Applied

15) Which are PRODUCTIVE conflict management strategies?

A) Avoid the conflict and use force.

B) Use silencers and gunnysack.

C) Fight actively and with argumentativeness.

D) Strategically manipulate the other person and fight with verbal aggressiveness.

Answer: C

Diff: 3   *Page Ref: 207-214*

Skill: Applied

TRUE/FALSE. Write 'T' if the statement is true and 'F' if the statement is false.

1) Even in a supportive environment, silence takes on a negative value.

Answer: FALSE
Diff: 2   Page Ref: 210
Skill: Interpretive

2) It is not so much the conflict that creates the problem as the way in which the individuals approach and deal with the conflict.

Answer: TRUE
Diff: 2   Page Ref: 202–205
Skill: Factual

3) Conflict can be avoided in any meaningful relationship.

Answer: FALSE
Diff: 2   Page Ref: 243–244
Skill: Factual

4) Most people generally agree on what conflict is and how it operates.

Answer: FALSE
Diff: 2   Page Ref: 242–244
Skill: Factual

5) Relationship conflicts are concerned with things external to the relationship itself.

Answer: FALSE
Diff: 2   Page Ref: 242
Skill: Factual

6) The major value of interpersonal conflict is that it forces the individuals to examine a problem and work toward a potential solution.

Answer: TRUE
Diff: 2   Page Ref: 244–245
Skill: Factual

7) A study by Kurdek showed that affectional orientation has much to do with the topics people argue about.

Answer: FALSE
Diff: 2   Page Ref: 202
Skill: Factual

8) Conflicts are usually all content or all relationship oriented.

Answer: FALSE
Diff: 2   *Page Ref: 201*
Skill: Factual

9) In Japan, it is especially important to embarrass in public the person with whom you have a conflict.

Answer: FALSE
Diff: 2   *Page Ref: 203*
Skill: Factual

10) Usually confronting a conflict indicates concern, commitment and a desire to preserve the relationship.

Answer: TRUE
Diff: 2   *Page Ref: 204–205*
Skill: Factual

11) Over 75% of both single and married couples reported that they had experienced physical violence in their relationship.

Answer: FALSE
Diff: 2   *Page Ref: 208–209*
Skill: Factual

12) The aim of a relationship conflict is to win and have your opponent lose.

Answer: FALSE
Diff: 3   *Page Ref: 201*
Skill: Factual

13) Men are more apt than women to use violent methods to achieve compliance.

Answer: TRUE
Diff: 2   *Page Ref: 208–209*
Skill: Factual

14) The aim of a relationship conflict is to resolve a problem and strengthen the relationship.

Answer: TRUE
Diff: 3   *Page Ref: 201*
Skill: Factual

15) After the conflict is over, the best thing to do is to forget about it.

Answer: FALSE
Diff: 2   *Page Ref: 216–217*
Skill: Factual

16) One of the most puzzling findings is that many victims of violence interpret it as a sign of love.

Answer: TRUE
Diff: 2   Page Ref: 209
Skill: Factual

17) Women are more apt to withdraw from a conflict situation than are men.

Answer: FALSE
Diff: 3   Page Ref: 206–207
Skill: Factual

18) Researchers note that both high and low argumentatives may experience communication difficulties.

Answer: TRUE
Diff: 2   Page Ref: 213–215
Skill: Factual

19) In a conflict situation, women are more apt than men to reveal their negative feelings.

Answer: TRUE
Diff: 3   Page Ref: 206–207
Skill: Factual

CHAPTER 12   Interviewing

MULTIPLE CHOICE. Choose the one alternative that best completes the statement or answers the question.

1) An advantage of team interviewing is that it
   A) gives the audience different view points on the interviewee.
   B) is expensive.
   C) may degenerate into what may appear like an interrogation.
   D) may focus too much on those conducting the interview.

Answer: A
Diff: 2   Page Ref: 230
Skill: Factual

2) When the general aim is to discover what the individual is doing well (and to praise it) and what the individual is doing poorly (and to correct it), the interview is most likely the
   A) persuasive interview.
   B) appraisal interview.
   C) exit interview.
   D) information interview.

Answer: B
Diff: 2   Page Ref: 223–224
Skill: Factual

3) "What would you do as a manager here?" This question dimension is best described as
   A) closed
   B) follow-up
   C) open
   D) indirect

Answer: C
Diff: 3   Page Ref: 221–223
Skill:

4) In the ABC Company a number of executives resigned to take positions with other firms. No one at ABC seems to have a firm grasp of why these people left and management now worries that this trend will continue. The ABC Company would do well to establish

   A) counseling interviews.

   B) appraisal interviews.

   C) persuasive interviews.

   D) exit interviews.

   Answer: D
   Diff: 2   *Page Ref: 223–224*
   Skill: Applied

5) Interviews with noted personalities, such as those who appear in popular magazines, are most clearly examples of

   A) informative interviews.

   B) persuasive interviews.

   C) appraisal interviews.

   D) exit interviews.

   Answer: A
   Diff: 2   *Page Ref: 223–224*
   Skill: Interpretive

6) When an interviewee's performance is assessed by management or by more experienced colleagues, the interview is most clearly an example of

   A) an informative interview.

   B) a persuasive interview.

   C) an appraisal interview.

   D) an exit interview.

   Answer: C
   Diff: 2   *Page Ref: 223–224*
   Skill: Applied

7) An interview designed to provide guidance and help a person cope more effectively with day-to-day living is most clearly an example of

   A) an appraisal interview.

   B) a counseling interview.

   C) a persuasive interview.

   D) an employment interview.

   Answer: B
   Diff: 2   *Page Ref: 223–224*
   Skill: Applied

8) In dealing with unlawful questions, the first strategy recommended by the author is to

   A) answer the part of the question you do not object to.

   B) tell the interviewer that the question is an unlawful one.

   C) ignore the question; act as if you did not hear it.

   D) lie.

   Answer: A
   Diff: 2   Page Ref: 233–235
   Skill: Factual

9) The four general interview structures include all of the following EXCEPT

   A) informal.

   B) guided.

   C) standard open.

   D) qualitative.

   Answer: D
   Diff: 2   Page Ref: 220–221
   Skill: Factual

10) Which is a guideline your author offers for conducting information interviews?

   A) tape the interview always

   B) close the interview with criticism

   C) ask closed questions

   D) prepare your questions

   Answer: D
   Diff: 3   Page Ref: 223–224
   Skill: Factual

11) Which is a reason for why people fail at interviews?

   A) they are prepared

   B) they have initiative

   C) they have poor listening skills

   D) they have pleasant personalities

   Answer: C
   Diff: 1   Page Ref: 232
   Skill: Factual

12) Which is a suggestion for communicating confidence?

    A) take a passive role in the interview

    B) avoid eye contact with the interviewer

    C) use vocalized pauses

    D) admit mistakes

Answer: D
Diff: 2   *Page Ref: 232*
Skill: Factual

13) Which question would be legal in a job interview in the USA

    A) Is Chinese your native language?

    B) Do you have a picture I can attach to your resume?

    C) Do you have any physical problems that might prevent you from fulfilling your responsibilities at this job?

    D) What is your affectional orientation?

Answer: C
Diff: 3   *Page Ref: 233-235*
Skill: Factual

14) Which is a benefit of talk shows?

    A) They promote the idea that communication will solve all problems.

    B) They have given a public platform to groups who have generally not had media exposure.

    C) They promote the idea that the more communication a couple has the better the relationship will be.

    D) They create the impression that the world is divided into two extremes.

Answer: B
Diff: 3   *Page Ref: 222*
Skill: Factual

TRUE/FALSE. Write 'T' if the statement is true and 'F' if the statement is false.

1) Interviewing is a particular form of interpersonal communication in which two persons interact largely by question-and-answer format for the purpose of achieving rather specific goals.

Answer: TRUE
Diff: 1   *Page Ref: 220*
Skill: Factual

2) The interview in which the interviewee's performance is assessed by management or by more experienced colleagues is called the employment interview.

Answer: FALSE
Diff: 2   *Page Ref: 223-224*
Skill: Interpretive

3) In employment interviews, all questions are legal.

Answer: FALSE
Diff: 1   *Page Ref: 233–235*
Skill: Interpretive

4) The interview is distinctly different from other forms of communication because it proceeds through questions and answers.

Answer: TRUE
Diff: 1   *Page Ref: 220*
Skill: Factual

5) We can distinguish the different types of interviews on the basis of the goals of interviewer and interviewees.

Answer: TRUE
Diff: 1   *Page Ref: 223*
Skill: Factual

6) All interviews contain elements of both information and persuasion.

Answer: TRUE
Diff: 1   *Page Ref: 220–224*
Skill: Interpretive

7) Spontaneity and making up the questions on the spot at an informational interview works best to make your questions not sound contrived.

Answer: FALSE
Diff: 2   *Page Ref: 224–225*
Skill: Interpretive

8) In an information interview, the use of questions which can be answered with "yes" and "no" answers are the best.

Answer: FALSE
Diff: 2   *Page Ref: 224–225*
Skill: Interpretive

9) At an employment interview, the interviewee should never ask any questions but rather should be polite by responding only when spoken to.

Answer: FALSE
Diff: 2   *Page Ref: 225–228*
Skill: Interpretive

10) In China, Japan, and Korea, it would be illegal to ask a job candidate if she or he is married.

Answer: FALSE
Diff: 2   *Page Ref: 232–233*
Skill: Factual

11) Since employment interviews are anxiety provoking, you're likely to experience some communication apprehension.

Answer: TRUE
Diff: 1   *Page Ref: 225–228*
Skill: Factual

12) A great number of jobs are won or lost on the basis of physical appearance alone.

Answer: TRUE
Diff: 1   *Page Ref: 230*
Skill: Factual

13) All interviews have specific objectives.

Answer: TRUE
Diff: 1   *Page Ref: 220–221*
Skill: Factual

14) One study found that a high number of "talkaholics" were majoring in journalism or communication.

Answer: TRUE
Diff: 1   *Page Ref: 226*
Skill: Factual

CHAPTER 13   Small Groups

MULTIPLE CHOICE. Choose the one alternative that best completes the statement or answers the question.

1) Among the rules for brainstorming, which is incorrect?
   A) Negative criticism is not allowed.
   B) Quality is desired.
   C) Combinations and extensions are desired.
   D) Freewheeling is wanted.

   Answer: B
   Diff: 2   Page Ref: 248
   Skill: Factual

2) A problem-solving discussion will probably be most productive if
   A) several solutions are posed at the beginning of the discussion.
   B) the broadest possible statement of the problem is made.
   C) approximately six steps are followed from defining the problem to testing the selected solutions.
   D) the discussion is approached with great flexibility.

   Answer: C
   Diff: 2   Page Ref: 252–255
   Skill: Factual

3) Advertisers who want to collect a wide variety of suggestions for an ad campaign should probably first engage in
   A) problem-solving discussion.
   B) brainstorming.
   C) personal growth discussion.
   D) educational or learning discussion.

   Answer: B
   Diff: 2   Page Ref: 248
   Skill: Interpretive

4) The first three steps in the problem-solving process are to
   A) define the problem, analyze the problem, and identify possible solutions.
   B) analyze the problem, establish criteria for evaluating solutions, and identify possible
      solutions.
   C) define and analyze the problem, establish criteria for evaluating solutions, and identify
      possible solutions.
   D) define the problem, identify possible solutions, and evaluate solutions.

   Answer: C
   Diff: 2   *Page Ref: 253*
   Skill: Factual

5) The members of XYZ Corporation arrange themselves in a circular or semicircular pattern and
   share the relevant information or attempt to solve the problem without any set pattern of
   identifying who speaks when. These members are using the small group format known as the
   A) round table.
   B) panel.
   C) symposium.
   D) symposium-forum.

   Answer: A
   Diff: 2   *Page Ref: 247*
   Skill: Interpretive

6) In their Credo for Free and Responsible Communication in a Democratic Society, the National
   Communication Association endorses which one of these principles?
   A) We take the concept of free speech symbolically.
   B) We reject the right to privacy.
   C) We urge the development of hardware and software that requires specialized,
      technological expertise.
   D) We urge designers and regulators of electronic forms of communication to use special
      vigilance to insure the works of individuals or groups are protected from unfair use by
      others.

   Answer: D
   Diff: 3   *Page Ref: 243*
   Skill: Factual

7) When you communicate with just one other person, in an Internet Relay Chat group, without
   giving access to your message to other participants, your activity is called
   A) lurking.
   B) whispering.
   C) empowering.
   D) IRC-ing.

   Answer: B
   Diff: 4   *Page Ref: 242-243*
   Skill: Factual

8) At a convention of the National Communication Association, one session consists of three or four speakers who each deliver a relatively prepared presentation, much like a public speech. After the speeches are presented, the audience asks questions of the speakers. This convention session most clearly follows the format known as the

A) round table.

B) panel.

C) symposium.

D) symposium-forum.

Answer: D

Diff: 2   Page Ref: 247

Skill: Applied

9) The forum part of a small group format refers most clearly to the

A) asking and answering of audience questions.

B) presentation of relatively prepared speeches.

C) use of experts as members of the group.

D) interaction of group members without any set pattern of speaking order.

Answer: A

Diff: 2   Page Ref: 247

Skill: Factual

10) The type of power that an older brother has over a younger brother because the younger brother wants to be like him is called

A) referent power.

B) legitimate power.

C) reward power.

D) coercive power.

E) expert power.

Answer: A

Diff: 2   Page Ref: 288-289

Skill: Interpretive

11) When your parents deny privileges concerning time or money, the type of power they are using is called

A) expert power.

B) coercive power.

C) reward power.

D) legitimate power.

Answer: B

Diff: 2   Page Ref: 246-247

Skill: Interpretive

12) This method of problem solving uses limited discussion and confidential voting to obtain a group decision.

    A) the Delphi method

    B) the nominal group technique

    C) the Omega technique

    D) the brainstorming formula

Answer: B
Diff: 2   *Page Ref: 255–256*
Skill: Factual

13) The small group problem-solving method that usually takes longer and generally wastes a considerable amount of time is

    A) the Delphi method.

    B) majority rule.

    C) consensus.

    D) brainstorming.

Answer: C
Diff: 2   *Page Ref: 258*
Skill: Interpretive

14) Which way can you communicate your power in a small group?

    A) Maintain a closed posture.

    B) Use adaptors.

    C) Never break eye contact.

    D) Respond visibly but in moderation.

Answer: D
Diff: 3   *Page Ref: 247*
Skill: Factual

15) Personal growth groups aim to

    A) discover what people think about an issue or product.

    B) have members pool their knowledge to the benefit of all.

    C) help members cope with particular difficulties.

    D) help people cope with the problems society confronts them with.

Answer: C
Diff: 3   *Page Ref: 249–250*
Skill: Factual

16) To evaluate solutions, de Bono provides you with six critical thinking hats. Which hat asks that you become the devil's advocate?

   A) the fact hat

   B) the negative argument hat

   C) the creative new idea hat

   D) the control of thinking hat

   Answer: B

   Diff: 2   Page Ref: 254

   Skill: Factual

17) Which is true of quality circles?

   A) The group reports its findings to no one.

   B) The motivation for establishing quality circles is to improve quality, profitability, and morale.

   C) Members are drawn randomly from any area in the organization.

   D) The only method used to investigate problems is face-to-face problem-solving.

   Answer: B

   Diff: 2   Page Ref: 256–257

   Skill: Factual

18) Your author suggests three questions for evaluating research. Which question is NOT suggested?

   A) Do the results justify the conclusion?

   B) Are the results valid?

   C) Are the results reliable?

   D) Are the results ethical?

   Answer: D

   Diff: 2   Page Ref: 255

   Skill: Factual

19) In this culture, you're expected to confront a group leader or supervisor or friend assertively.

   A) high power distance culture

   B) user-friendly cultures

   C) low power distance cultures

   D) gatekeeping cultures

   Answer: C

   Diff: 3   Page Ref: 249

   Skill: Factual

20) Which is an "idea killer" or "killer message"?

   A) It will work.

   B) It is logical.

   C) What we have is good enough.

   D) It is possible.

   Answer: C
   Diff: 2   Page Ref: 251
   Skill: Factual

21) A useful skill for listening to new ideas, derived from Carl Rogers, is PIP'N. Which term is NOT a part of this acronym?

   A) paraphrase

   B) insecurity

   C) positive

   D) negative

   Answer: B
   Diff: 2   Page Ref: 257
   Skill: Factual

TRUE/FALSE. Write 'T' if the statement is true and 'F' if the statement is false.

1) According to the definition of a group presented by the author, people attending a rock concert would not constitute a small group.

   Answer: TRUE
   Diff: 1   Page Ref: 239
   Skill: Interpretive

2) A common purpose among the members is an essential aspect of the definition of a group.

   Answer: TRUE
   Diff: 1   Page Ref: 239-240
   Skill: Factual

3) Organization or structure among the members is essential if these members are to constitute a group.

   Answer: TRUE
   Diff: 1   Page Ref: 239-241
   Skill: Factual

4) Proximity--the physical closeness of the members--is an essential aspect of the definition of a group.

   Answer: FALSE
   Diff: 1   Page Ref: 239-240
   Skill: Interpretive

5) Everyone is a member of a wide variety of small groups.

Answer: TRUE
Diff: 1   *Page Ref: 239–241*
Skill: Factual

6) Many groups develop into kinds of small cultures with their own norms.

Answer: TRUE
Diff: 2   *Page Ref: 240–241*
Skill: Factual

7) Norms tell members of a group how to behave with acceptable and appropriate behaviors.

Answer: TRUE
Diff: 1   *Page Ref: 240–241*
Skill: Factual

8) Norms are always explicit and never implicit.

Answer: FALSE
Diff: 2   *Page Ref: 240–241*
Skill: Factual

9) Power permeates all small groups and in fact all relationships.

Answer: TRUE
Diff: 1   *Page Ref: 244*
Skill: Factual

10) IRC communication takes place in real time.

Answer: TRUE
Diff: 2   *Page Ref: 242–243*
Skill: Factual

11) Groups differ in the types of power that the members use and the types to which they respond.

Answer: TRUE
Diff: 2   *Page Ref: 244–247*
Skill: Factual

12) Some evidence shows that individual brainstorming can work even more effectively than group brainstorming.

Answer: TRUE
Diff: 2   *Page Ref: 249*
Skill: Factual

13) Expert power wields power over others because the power holder has the ability to administer punishments to or remove rewards from the other person.

Answer: FALSE
Diff: 2   *Page Ref: 246*
Skill: Interpretive

14) In the Delphi method, one of the most important factors in the success of using this method is the face-to-face interaction.

Answer: FALSE
Diff: 1   *Page Ref: 256*
Skill: Factual

15) One disadvantage of majority rule is that it can lead to factioning, where minorities align against the majority.

Answer: TRUE
Diff: 2   *Page Ref: 258*
Skill: Factual

16) The group operating under consensus reaches a decision only when all group members agree.

Answer: TRUE
Diff: 1   *Page Ref: 258*
Skill: Factual

17) The media, usually on the basis of their own codes and sometimes because of legal regulations, censors what gets through to viewers.

Answer: TRUE
Diff: 2   *Page Ref: 245*
Skill: Factual

ESSAY. Write your answer in the space provided or on a separate sheet of paper.

1) Write your answer in the space provided or on a separate sheet of paper. Explain how you would combat idea killers (that is, killer messages). Respond to the killer messages your author provides.
Answer: Answers will vary.
Diff: 2   *Page Ref: 251*
Skill: Applied

2) Explain and apply the PIP'N technique to some new idea you have just heard.
Answer: Answers will vary.
Diff: 3   *Page Ref: 257*
Skill: Applied

3) Identify and discuss four different gatekeepers.

Answer: Answers will vary.

Diff: 3   *Page Ref: 245*

Skill: Applied

CHAPTER 14   Members and Leaders

MULTIPLE CHOICE. Choose the one alternative that best completes the statement or answers the question.

1) The initiator–contributor, information giver, elaborator, and coordinator are best defined as
   A) group task roles.
   B) group building roles.
   C) "individual" roles.
   D) maintenance roles.

   Answer: A
   Diff: 2   *Page Ref: 261–262*
   Skill: Factual

2) In this group task role, the member summarizes what has been said and addresses the direction the group is taking.
   A) elaborator
   B) coordinator
   C) orienter
   D) energizer

   Answer: C
   Diff: 3   *Page Ref: 261–262*
   Skill: Factual

3) The gatekeeper–expediter, the standard setter or ego ideal, and the observer and commentator are best defined as
   A) group task roles.
   B) group building and maintenance roles.
   C) "individual" roles.
   D) dysfunctional roles.

   Answer: B
   Diff: 2   *Page Ref: 261–262*
   Skill: Factual

4) In this group building and maintenance role, the member mediates the various differences between group members.
   A) encourager
   B) harmonizer
   C) compromiser
   D) follower

   Answer: A
   Diff: 2   *Page Ref: 261–262*
   Skill: Factual

5) "Individual" (or dysfunctional) roles would include
   A) opinion seeker, opinion giver, orienter.
   B) encourager, harmonizer, follower.
   C) aggressor, blocker, recognition seeker.
   D) compromiser, commentator, ego ideal.

   Answer: C
   Diff: 2   *Page Ref: 261–262*
   Skill: Factual

6) In this individual role group, the member provides negative feedback, is disagreeable, and opposes other members or suggestions regardless of their merit.
   A) aggressor
   B) playboy/playgirl
   C) special–interest pleader
   D) blocker

   Answer: D
   Diff: 3   *Page Ref: 261–262*
   Skill: Factual

7) In interaction process analysis, the natural opposite of the social–emotional positive category is which of the following?
   A) shows solidarity
   B) shows disagreement
   C) shows tension release
   D) gives suggestions

   Answer: B
   Diff: 2   *Page Ref: 262–263*
   Skill: Factual

8) In interaction process analysis, the natural opposite of the questions category is which of the following?
   A) asks for suggestions
   B) shows tension
   C) gives information
   D) asks for opinions

   Answer: C
   Diff: 2   *Page Ref: 262–263*
   Skill: Factual

9) Which is the best way to handle conflict in small groups?
   A) Center conflict on personalities rather than on issues.
   B) When you disagree, make it clear your disagreement is with the person rather than the ideas expressed.
   C) When someone disagrees with you, take the disagreement as a personal attack.
   D) When you disagree, make it clear your disagreement is with the solution suggested rather than with the person who expressed them.

   Answer: D
   Diff: 3   *Page Ref: 263*
   Skill: Interpretive

10) In being critically open-minded, the author suggests this about problem solving small group meetings.
    A) Members should come to a meeting with their minds already made up.
    B) Members should be unwilling to alter or revise their suggestions after discussion occurs.
    C) Members should be judiciously open-minded.
    D) Members should accept or reject any suggestions without critically evaluating them.

    Answer: C
    Diff: 2   *Page Ref: 264*
    Skill: Interpretive

11) Pat expresses frequent negative evaluations of the actions of group members, is disagreeable, and boasts. In these behaviors Pat is serving primarily
    A) group task roles.
    B) group building roles.
    C) "individual" roles.
    D) group maintenance roles.

    Answer: C
    Diff: 2   *Page Ref: 261–262*
    Skill: Applied

12) The information seeker, initiator–contributor, information giver, and coordinator are most clearly

   A) group task roles.
   B) group building roles.
   C) group maintenance roles.
   D) "individual" roles.

   Answer: A
   Diff: 2   *Page Ref: 261–262*
   Skill: Factual

13) Among the functions of a leader in small group communication are all of the following EXCEPT

   A) to keep members on the track.
   B) to encourage ongoing evaluation and improvement.
   C) to prepare group members for the discussion.
   D) to publicize the decisions of the group members.

   Answer: D
   Diff: 2   *Page Ref: 264–265*
   Skill: Factual

14) Among the characteristics of groupthink are all of the following behaviors EXCEPT

   A) the group limits its discussion of possible alternatives to only a small range.
   B) once the group has made a decision, it does not reexamine its decisions even when there are indications of possible dangers.
   C) the group is unselective in the information that it seriously considers.
   D) the group makes little effort to obtain expert information even from people within their own organization.

   Answer: C
   Diff: 3   *Page Ref: 264*
   Skill: Factual

15) Which of the following is NOT considered a symptom of groupthink?

   A) Group members think that the group and its members are invulnerable to dangers.
   B) Group members believe their group is immoral.
   C) Group pressure is on any member who expresses doubts or questions the group's arguments or proposals.
   D) Members create rationalizations to avoid dealing directly with warnings or threats.

   Answer: B
   Diff: 2   *Page Ref: 264*
   Skill: Factual

16) At its meetings, the Department of Communication faculty members view themselves as invulnerable to dangers. They censor their own doubts and believe their members are always in unanimous agreement. In these behaviors, this department displays symptoms of

A) agreement preoccupation.

B) gatekeeping.

C) consensus syndrome.

D) groupthink.

Answer: D

Diff: 2   Page Ref: 264

Skill: Applied

17) The characteristics of a good leader include all of the following EXCEPT

A) controls personal moods.

B) sticks closely to the task at hand.

C) praises group members and their contributions publicly.

D) does what others are expected to do.

Answer: B

Diff: 2   Page Ref: 270–274

Skill: Factual

18) In this approach to leadership, a leader is one who enables and empowers group members.

A) traits approach

B) functional approach

C) transformational approach

D) situational approach

Answer: C

Diff: 2   Page Ref: 265–266

Skill: Factual

19) In this approach to leadership, a leader is one who balances task accomplishment and member satisfaction on the basis of the unique situation.

A) transformational approach

B) traits approach

C) functional approach

D) situational approach

Answer: D

Diff: 2   Page Ref: 265–266

Skill: Factual

20) In this style of leadership, you provide direction but allow the group to develop and progress the way its members wish.

A) authoritarian

B) democratic

C) laissez-faire

D) charismatic

Answer: B

Diff: 2   Page Ref: 269

Skill: Factual

21) In this style of leadership, you determine the group policies or make decisions without consulting or securing agreement from the members.

A) authoritarian

B) laissez-faire

C) charismatic

D) laissez-faire

Answer: A

Diff: 2   Page Ref: 269

Skill: Factual

22) In this style of leadership, you would take no initiative in directing or suggesting alternative courses of action.

A) democratic

B) charismatic

C) laissez-faire

D) authoritarian

Answer: C

Diff: 2   Page Ref: 269

Skill: Factual

23) What is true about group agendas?

A) The more formal the group, the less important the agenda becomes.

B) The agenda need not be agreed upon by group members.

C) An agenda is a list of the tasks the group wishes to complete.

D) In formal business groups, the agenda will be neither detailed nor explicit.

Answer: C

Diff: 3   Page Ref: 270

Skill: Factual

24) One way a leader may empower group members is to

    A) discourage growth.

    B) keep decision–making power and authority to himself or herself.

    C) lower their self–esteem.

    D) be constructively critical.

Answer: D
Diff: 2   Page Ref: 271
Skill: Factual

25) Which of the following is a procedural conflict?

    A) One member dominates the group.

    B) Disagreement over who is in charge.

    C) Several members battle for control.

    D) Some members refuse to participate.

Answer: B
Diff: 3   Page Ref: 272
Skill: Factual

26) Which is NOT a principle of conflict management?

    A) Preserve the dignity and respect of all members.

    B) Value diversity and differences.

    C) Listen critically.

    D) Seek out and emphasize common ground.

Answer: C
Diff: 2   Page Ref: 273
Skill: Factual

27) Which will NOT facilitate small group communication with the deaf?

    A) Slow down the pace of communication slightly.

    B) Use hands–on experience whenever possible in training situations.

    C) Avoid using visual aids.

    D) Seat the deaf person to his or her best advantage.

Answer: C
Diff: 2   Page Ref: 274
Skill: Factual

28) Which is NOT true of effective leaders?

A) They praise others and their contributions publicly.

B) They criticize sparingly, constructively, and courteously.

C) They work hard at understanding the wants and concerns of others.

D) They admit errors only when they must.

Answer: D
Diff: 2   Page Ref: 274-277
Skill: Factual

29) In American culture one might voice disagreement and be influenced by a belief that "the squeaky wheel gets the grease." In Asian culture, one might not voice disagreement and be influenced, according to your author, by which of these beliefs?

A) When in doubt, do something.

B) Be willing to make decisions.

C) The protruding nail gets pounded down.

D) You must wear your learning like a watch.

Answer: C
Diff: 2   Page Ref: 175-277
Skill: Interpretive

30) One study showed that most people will be more influenced by speakers using task not dominance cues. Which is a task cue?

A) Using a relatively rapid speech rate.

B) Pointing fingers.

C) Maintaining rigid posture.

D) Speaking in a loud and angry voice.

Answer: A
Diff: 3   Page Ref: 272
Skill: Applied

31) What can we NOT learn from Attila the Hun?

A) empathy

B) indecisiveness

C) accountability

D) loyalty

Answer: A
Diff: 3   Page Ref: 271
Skill: Factual

32) What is true about the agenda-setting theory of the media?

    A) The media tell people what to think.

    B) The media do not tell people what to think about.

    C) The media have the ability to select and call ideas and events to the attention of the public.

    D) The media serve the public with no agenda at all.

Answer: C
Diff: 3   *Page Ref: 273*
Skill: Interpretive

TRUE/FALSE. Write 'T' if the statement is true and 'F' if the statement is false.

1) The authoritarian leader provides direction but allows the group to develop and progress the way that the members wish.

Answer: FALSE
Diff: 2   *Page Ref: 269*
Skill: Factual

2) The laissez-faire leader determines the group policies or makes decisions without consulting or securing agreement from the group members.

Answer: FALSE
Diff: 2   *Page Ref: 269*
Skill: Factual

3) The democratic leader allows the group to develop and progress on its own and even allows it to make its own mistakes; this leader gives up or denies any real leadership authority.

Answer: FALSE
Diff: 2   *Page Ref: 269*
Skill: Factual

4) Individual roles are often considered dysfunctional in small group communication.

Answer: TRUE
Diff: 2   *Page Ref: 262*
Skill: Factual

5) One symptom of groupthink occurs when group members emerge whose function it is to filter the information that gets to other members of the group, especially when such information may create diversity of opinion.

Answer: TRUE
Diff: 2   *Page Ref: 264*
Skill: Factual

6) When all members are about equal and concerned about their individual rights, authoritarian leadership is best.

Answer: FALSE
Diff: 2   *Page Ref: 269*
Skill: Factual

7) When speed and efficiency are paramount, laissez-faire leadership is best.

Answer: FALSE
Diff: 2   *Page Ref: 269*
Skill: Factual

8) Contemporary theorists on leadership favor the traits leader.

Answer: FALSE
Diff: 2   *Page Ref: 265*
Skill: Interpretive

9) Another name for individual roles are "dysfunctional roles."

Answer: TRUE
Diff: 2   *Page Ref: 262*
Skill: Factual

10) Solo performances hinder the group.

Answer: TRUE
Diff: 2   *Page Ref: 262*
Skill: Interpretive

11) The member who talks the least usually emerges as leader.

Answer: FALSE
Diff: 2   *Page Ref: 262*
Skill: Factual

12) Some researchers view the effective leader as one whose communications prevent the group from natural but unproductive diversions.

Answer: TRUE
Diff: 2   *Page Ref: 264-266*
Skill: Interpretive

ESSAY. Write your answer in the space provided or on a separate sheet of paper.

1) Write your answer in the space provided or on a separate sheet of paper. Identify and discuss four symptoms of group think.

Answer: Answers will vary.

Diff: 2   *Page Ref: 264*

Skill: Interpretive

2) In What is a Leader? (in table 14.2), pick one of the four approaches to leadership and explain why you prefer it.

Answer: Answers will vary.

Diff: 3   *Page Ref: 266*

Skill: Applied

CHAPTER 15   Topic, Audience, and Research

MULTIPLE CHOICE. Choose the one alternative that best completes the statement or answers the question.

1) Which of these statements is true?

A) The art of public speaking has failed to grow and develop since Aristotle wrote on it.

B) Aristotle, who taught in Rome during the first century, built an entire educational system based on the development of the effective and responsible orator.

C) Ethics is an integral part of all public speaking for speaker, listener, and critic.

D) It is in the public speaking situation that apprehension is least common and least severe.

Answer: C
Diff: 3   Page Ref: 280-282
Skill: Factual

2) There are five factors that contribute to speaker apprehension. Which is NOT a factor?

A) Facing new and different situations.

B) Seeing yourself as having superior status.

C) Lacking similarity with your audience.

D) Having a prior history of apprehension.

Answer: B
Diff: 3   Page Ref: 282-283
Skill: Factual

3) Systematic desensitization is a technique for dealing with a variety of fears including those involved in public speaking. According to your author, which is the least fearful behavior of the following?

A) Giving a speech in class

B) Answering a question in class

C) Introducing another speaker to the class

D) Asking a question in class

Answer: D
Diff: 2   Page Ref: 283
Skill: Factual

4) According to your author, which of these eases or lessens apprehension?

   A) Pretend you are a giant.

   B) Think of the audience as a group of children.

   C) Use a visual aid.

   D) Pretend the audience is naked.

   Answer: C
   Diff: 2   Page Ref: 282-284
   Skill: Factual

5) According to your author, which chemicals relieve rather create speaking tension?

   A) tranquilizers

   B) alcohol

   C) artificial stimulants

   D) all of the above

   E) none of the above

   Answer: E
   Diff: 2   Page Ref: 284
   Skill: Factual

6) In many Arab, Asian, and African cultures, discussing sex in an audience of both men and women would be considered obscene and offensive whereas in Scandinavia, sex is expected to be discussed openly and without embarrassment. This is especially suitable to which feature of a speech topic?

   A) The topic should be worthwhile.

   B) The topic should be sensitive and appropriate to the culture in which the speech takes place.

   C) The topic should deal with matters of substance.

   D) The topic should be morally conservative.

   Answer: B
   Diff: 3   Page Ref: 285-294
   Skill: Applied

7) TOPOI (or the system of topics) is a technique that involves asking questions about your general topic. Which questions does your author suggest?

   A) How much? How often? Who?

   B) What? Why? So what? Who cares?

   C) Who? What? Why? When? Where? How? So?

   D) Is it possible? Is it necessary? Is it affordable? Is it useful? Is it practical?

   Answer: C
   Diff: 2   Page Ref: 287
   Skill: Factual

8) Which is, according to the author, NOT usually seen as an aim of informative speeches?

    A) to clarify

    B) to change behavior

    C) to enlighten

    D) to define a concept

    Answer: B
    Diff: 2   *Page Ref: 288-289*
    Skill: Factual

9) Which purpose statement is the most specific?

    A) To persuade my audience to be generous.

    B) To persuade my audience to contribute a book to the next local library fund raiser.

    C) To persuade my audience to contribute to a cause.

    D) To persuade my audience to contribute a book.

    Answer: B
    Diff: 2   *Page Ref: 288-289*
    Skill: Interpretive

10) This refers to your tendency to act for or against a person, object, or position.

    A) attitude

    B) belief

    C) value

    D) disposition

    Answer: A
    Diff: 2   *Page Ref: 290*
    Skill: Factual

11) Your author lists four major sociological variables for analyzing your audience. Which is NOT one of them?

    A) culture

    B) age

    C) intelligence

    D) religion

    Answer: C
    Diff: 2   *Page Ref: 290-292*
    Skill: Factual

12) Which is a suggestion to help change your listeners from unwilling to willing?

    A) Organize your speech inductively.

    B) Build on commonalities.

    C) Don't talk down to your audience.

    D) Reward the audience for their attendance and attention.

Answer: D
Diff: 3   *Page Ref: 292*
Skill: Factual

13) Which is a suggestion to help change your listeners from unfavorable to favorable?

    A) Clear up any possible misapprehensions that may be causing the disagreement.

    B) Don't confuse a lack of knowledge with a lack of intelligence.

    C) Emphasize your credibility.

    D) Secure their interest and attention as early in your speech as possible.

Answer: A
Diff: 3   *Page Ref: 293*
Skill: Factual

14) These are discussion forums for the exchange of ideas on a wide variety of topics.

    A) e-mail

    B) newsgroups

    C) World Wide Web

    D) search engine

Answer: B
Diff: 2   *Page Ref: 296*
Skill: Factual

15) A list of subjects or categories of web links.

    A) search engine

    B) database

    C) directory

    D) almanac

Answer: C
Diff: 2   *Page Ref: 298*
Skill: Factual

16) The accounts occur in magazines and are simplified versions of rather complex issues written for the general public rather than for an audience of professional researchers.

A) academic research

B) general interest articles

C) almanacs

D) indexes

Answer: B
Diff: 3   Page Ref: 300
Skill: Factual

17) This index has available almost 200 magazines, newspapers, and journals that might be labeled "radical."

A) LEXIS

B) NEXIS

C) Readers Guide to Periodical Literature

D) Alternative Press Index

Answer: D
Diff: 2   Page Ref: 300–301
Skill: Factual

18) Your author offers all of these questions to help you critically evaluate research EXCEPT

A) Is the information politically correct?

B) Is the information current?

C) Is the information fair and unbiased?

D) Is the evidence reliable and the reasoning logical?

Answer: A
Diff: 2   Page Ref: 301–303
Skill: Factual

19) Your author asks you to AVOID one of the following when integrating your research into your speech.

A) Smooth transitions between your words and the words of an author you are citing.

B) Signal verbs such as "has found that," "argues that," or "wonders if."

C) Useless expressions such as "I want to quote an example here."

D) Acknowledging your source if you are only following the organizational structure of that source.

Answer: C
Diff: 3   Page Ref: 304
Skill: Factual

20) Which of the following statements about ethics in communication is NOT true?

   A) Ethics is a crucial consideration in all communications.

   B) Unethical statements have a potentially low level effect on the audience.

   C) Plagiarism is an example of unethical communication.

   D) Most people do not agree on what is ethical and what is unethical.

   Answer: B
   Diff: 2   Page Ref: 281–282
   Skill: Factual

21) Dissimilarity can best be described as

   A) feeling weird about your speech topic.

   B) feeling that you are the center of attention.

   C) feeling anxiety because of the differences in situations.

   D) the degree of difference you feel about your relationship to your audience.

   Answer: D
   Diff: 2   Page Ref: 290–294
   Skill: Interpretive

22) Using a combination of logical, ethical, and emotional appeals is a contribution from
   _____ to the study of public speaking.

   A) psychology

   B) classical rhetoric

   C) sociology

   D) interpersonal communication

   Answer: B
   Diff: 1   Page Ref: 280–281
   Skill: Factual

23) A speaker whose topic is medicare would have to be particularly sensitive to the
   _____ of the audience.

   A) gender breakdown

   B) age range

   C) subcultural differences

   D) sexual preferences

   Answer: B
   Diff: 2   Page Ref: 291
   Skill: Interpretive

24) Which one of the following statements about the nine steps of speech preparation reflects the views expressed in the text?

A) The speaker must follow these steps in a sequential order.

B) These steps are all the speaker will ever need to know about effective speech presentation.

C) As the speaker proceeds, s/he may need to go back to modify the material based on information developed in later steps.

D) If the speaker doesn't get enough information about the audience, this consideration can be eliminated from the speech preparation.

Answer: C
Diff: 2   Page Ref:
Skill: Interpretive

TRUE/FALSE. Write 'T' if the statement is true and 'F' if the statement is false.

1) "Ethics" refers to the morality of an act.

Answer: TRUE
Diff: 1   Page Ref: 281–282
Skill: Factual

2) Ethics is an integral part of all public speaking.

Answer: TRUE
Diff: 1   Page Ref: 281–282
Skill: Factual

3) Communication apprehension is most common and severe in public speaking.

Answer: TRUE
Diff: 1   Page Ref: 282–283
Skill: Factual

4) The first part of performance visualization is to develop a positive attitude and self-perception.

Answer: TRUE
Diff: 2   Page Ref: 283
Skill: Factual

5) Systematic desensitization is a technique for dealing exclusively with those involved in public speaking.

Answer: FALSE
Diff: 2   Page Ref: 283
Skill: Factual

6) Jack Valenti says the most effective way to lessen stage fright is "total, slavish, monkish preparation."

Answer: TRUE
Diff: 1   *Page Ref: 282-284*
Skill: Factual

7) By taking deep breaths before getting up to speak, you will make your body tense.

Answer: FALSE
Diff: 1   *Page Ref: 282-284*
Skill: Interpretive

8) Fear increases when you feel that the audience's expectations are very low.

Answer: FALSE
Diff: 2   *Page Ref: 282-284*
Skill: Interpretive

9) The two major purposes of public speeches are to inform and to persuade.

Answer: TRUE
Diff: 1   *Page Ref: 288*
Skill: Factual

10) After you have established your specific purpose, identify your general purpose.

Answer: FALSE
Diff: 2   *Page Ref: 288-289*
Skill: Factual

11) The persuasive speech does not have to go beyond simply providing information.

Answer: FALSE
Diff: 2   *Page Ref: 288-289*
Skill: Factual

12) "Value" refers to the confidence you have in the truth of some proposition.

Answer: FALSE
Diff: 2   *Page Ref: 290*
Skill: Factual

13) A listserv is an e-mail list of several to perhaps hundreds of people who exchange messages on a relatively specific topic at a rate of perhaps several to hundreds a week.

Answer: TRUE
Diff: 2   *Page Ref: 296*
Skill: Factual

14) Your author advises you to read the FAQs on your listserv to avoid asking questions that have already been answered.

Answer: TRUE
Diff: 2   *Page Ref: 296*
Skill: Factual

15) Primary source material includes summaries of the research appearing in popular magazines and television news reports on a corporation's earnings.

Answer: FALSE
Diff: 2   *Page Ref: 302*
Skill: Factual

16) Only a select few can "publish" on the Internet.

Answer: FALSE
Diff: 1   *Page Ref: 297–298*
Skill: Factual

17) Inaccurate news reports never creep into respected sources, such as *TIME* magazine or *The Boston Globe*.

Answer: FALSE
Diff: 2   *Page Ref: 299–300*
Skill: Factual

18) Your author advises you to avoid "signal verbs."

Answer: FALSE
Diff: 2   *Page Ref: 304*
Skill: Factual

19) The very first step in speech preparation is to conduct audience analysis.

Answer: FALSE
Diff: 1   *Page Ref: 285*
Skill: Interpretive

20) The purpose is the essence of what you want your audience to get out of your speech.

Answer: FALSE
Diff: 1   *Page Ref: 288–289*
Skill: Factual

21) Public speaking does not have to be face-to-face.

Answer: TRUE
Diff: 1   *Page Ref: 280–281*
Skill: Factual

22) In your initial public speaking efforts, you should strive to eliminate all speaker apprehension.

Answer: FALSE
Diff: 1   *Page Ref: 282–284*
Skill: Factual

23) Speaker apprehension is normal.

Answer: TRUE
Diff: 1   *Page Ref: 282–284*
Skill: Factual

24) Speaker apprehension is inevitably detrimental to the speaker.

Answer: FALSE
Diff: 1   *Page Ref: 282–284*
Skill: Factual

CHAPTER 16   Supporting and Organizing Your Speech

MULTIPLE CHOICE. Choose the one alternative that best completes the statement or answers the question.

1) Which thesis statement does your author favor over the others?
   A) The European economic unit, the EURO, will bankrupt the US and create World War III.
   B) Universities and colleges should be funded by the government of the US and by all NATO governments.
   C) Animal experimentation should be banned.
   D) Animal experimentation should be funded and companies funding it should receive a total tax credit.

   Answer: C
   Diff: 2   Page Ref: 308
   Skill: Interpretive

2) Which guideline is suggested to help you make the right decision about when to introduce your thesis?
   A) In a persuasive speech where your audience is hostile to your position, state your thesis early, clearly, and directly.
   B) In an informative speech, delay stating your thesis until you have moved your audience closer to your position.
   C) In a persuasive speech, when speaking to Asian cultures, make your point ask your audience directly to comply with your thesis.
   D) In a persuasive speech where your audience is neutral or positive, state your thesis explicitly and early in your speech.

   Answer: D
   Diff: 3   Page Ref: 308
   Skill: Factual

3) Your author suggests that you shorten your list of main points in a speech in all of the following ways EXCEPT:
   A) eliminate those points that seem least important to your thesis.
   B) select points that are most relevant to or that interest your audience.
   C) use five, six, or seven main points.
   D) combine those points that have a common focus.

   Answer: C
   Diff: 3   Page Ref: 311
   Skill: Factual

4) In supporting your propositions, this form of support is useful for adding spice and wit as well as authority to your speeches.
   A) definitions
   B) repetitions
   C) quotations
   D) comparisons and contrasts
   Answer: C
   Diff: 2   Page Ref: 310
   Skill: Factual

5) With respect to this form of support, your author cautions you to make sure they are relatively short, easily understood, and directly related to your point.
   A) definitions
   B) comparisons and contracts
   C) facts
   D) quotations
   Answer: D
   Diff: 2   Page Ref: 310
   Skill: Factual

6) This source for supporting your propositions refers to the opinions of experts or to the accounts of witnesses.
   A) examples
   B) narration
   C) statistics
   D) testimony
   Answer: D
   Diff: 2   Page Ref: 311–312
   Skill: Factual

7) This narrative provides examples of excellence, examples to follow or admire.
   A) explanatory narrative
   B) exemplary narrative
   C) persuasive narrative
   D) hortatory narrative
   Answer: B
   Diff: 2   Page Ref: 311
   Skill: Factual

8) As a general rule (to which there are many exceptions), the best presentation aid is
    A) a model.
    B) a graph.
    C) a word chart.
    D) the object itself.
    E) a map.

Answer: D
Diff: 1   *Page Ref: 314–316*
Skill: Factual

9) This medium of presentation is helpful in showing a series of visuals that may be of very different types (for example, photographs, illustrations, or tables).
    A) chalkboard
    B) flip charts
    C) slides and transparency projections
    D) handouts

Answer: C
Diff: 2   *Page Ref: 317*
Skill: Factual

10) Which is a guideline your author offers for using presentation aids?
    A) Test the aids before using them.
    B) Know your aids in a general way.
    C) Integrate your aids into your speech visibly.
    D) Talk to your aid.

Answer: A
Diff: 2   *Page Ref: 319*
Skill: Factual

11) Computer presentation software enables you to print out all of the following handouts EXCEPT
    A) the slides shown during your speech.
    B) the slides plus speaker notes.
    C) the slides plus places for listeners to write notes next to each of them.
    D) all of the above
    E) none of the above

Answer: D
Diff: 2   *Page Ref: 322–323*
Skill: Factual

223

12) In developing your slides, your author suggests which of the following?

   A) Put one complete thought on a slide.

   B) Put long passages of text on a slide.

   C) Use a sans serif type for text and a serif type for headings.

   D) Use a major statement and five or more subordinated (bulleted) phrases.

   Answer: A
   Diff: 3   Page Ref: 317
   Skill: Factual

13) A speech on important cities or religions of the world might best be organized into this pattern.

   A) temporal

   B) problem–solution

   C) topical

   D) cause–effect/effect–cause

   Answer: C
   Diff: 2   Page Ref: 325
   Skill: Applied

14) A speech in which you try to convince your audience that jury awards for damages should be limited might best be organized into this pattern.

   A) cause–effect/effect–cause

   B) problem–solution

   C) topical

   D) temporal

   Answer: B
   Diff: 2   Page Ref: 325–326
   Skill: Applied

15) Which is the correct order for the steps in the motivated sequence pattern of speech arrangement?

   A) Need, satisfaction, attention, action, visualization

   B) visualization, action, need, attention, satisfaction

   C) attention, need, satisfaction, visualization, action

   D) attention, visualization, need, action, satisfaction

   Answer: C
   Diff: 2   Page Ref: 326
   Skill: Factual

16) In this step of the motivated sequence, the speaker tells the audience what they should do to ensure that the need is satisfied as visualized.

  A) attention

  B) satisfaction

  C) need

  D) action

  Answer: D

  Diff: 2   Page Ref: 326

  Skill: Factual

17) In this step of the motivated sequence, you fulfill the need by presenting the "answer" or the "solution" to the need you demonstrated.

  A) visualization

  B) action

  C) satisfaction

  D) attention

  Answer: C

  Diff: 2   Page Ref: 326

  Skill: Factual

18) This organizational pattern is useful in information speeches in which you want to explain objectively the pros and the cons of each plan, method, or product.

  A) structure–function

  B) advantages–disadvantages

  C) claim and proof

  D) multiple definition

  Answer: B

  Diff: 2   Page Ref: 327

  Skill: Applied

19) This organizational pattern is especially useful in a persuasive speech in which you want to prove the truth or usefulness of a particular proposition.

  A) Who? What? Why? Where? When?

  B) multiple definition

  C) claim and proof

  D) structure-function

  Answer: C

  Diff: 2   Page Ref: 327–328

  Skill: Applied

20) Which is offered as a way of gaining the attention of your audience?

   A) Refer to audience members.

   B) Avoid humor and remain serious.

   C) Cite well known facts or statistics.

   D) Make statements and avoid questions.

   Answer: A
   Diff: 2   Page Ref: 328–329
   Skill: Factual

21) To establish a speaker-audience-topic relationship and answer your listener's question about why they should listen to you speak on this topic, which is suggested?

   A) Express dissimilarities with the audience.

   B) Ignore the occasion.

   C) Criticize the audience.

   D) Establish your competence in the subject.

   Answer: D
   Diff: 2   Page Ref: 328–329
   Skill: Factual

22) Your conclusion can serve all of the following EXCEPT

   A) to orient the audience.

   B) to summarize.

   C) to motivate.

   D) to provide closure.

   Answer: A
   Diff: 2   Page Ref: 328–329
   Skill: Factual

23) This transitional function signals your organizational structure through which stylistic device?

   A) However, also consider....

   B) Therefore,...

   C) In conclusion,...

   D) I'll first explain the problems with the jury awards and then propose a workable solution.

   Answer: D
   Diff: 3   Page Ref: 330
   Skill: Applied

24) This transitional function signals the part of your speech you're approaching through which stylistic devise?
   A) Now, let's discuss why we're here today.
   B) So, as you can see...
   C) If you want further evidence, look at...
   D) A second argument...

   Answer: A
   Diff: 3   Page Ref: 330
   Skill: Applied

25) What is true about culture and message organization?
   A) Speakers in Japan need to make their points very obvious and very direct to keep from insulting their listeners.
   B) Speakers in the United States are expected to lead their listeners to a conclusion through example, illustration, and other indirect means.
   C) American culture requires many ideas to be considered in the same paragraph in an essage or in the same part of a speech.
   D) In the United States, each major proposition of a speech or written composition should be fully developed before the speaker or writer move on to the next point.

   Answer: D
   Diff: 3   Page Ref: 311–313
   Skill: Factual

26) Presenting_____ helps the audience to understand any specialized terms that may otherwise be too vague or abstract.
   A) examples
   B) illustrations
   C) testimony
   D) definitions

   Answer: D
   Diff: 1   Page Ref: 328
   Skill: Factual

27) When speaking about the various majors in college, the speaker may divide the topic into equal subtopics. This organizational pattern is known as:
   A) temporal
   B) topical
   C) problem–solution
   D) transactional

   Answer: B
   Diff: 2   Page Ref: 325–327
   Skill: Factual

28) The speech introduction should be written last because:
   A) the speaker must know what is going to be said in the speech before preparing the introduction.
   B) it is the most difficult and time–consuming to write.
   C) it is not as important as the conclusion of the speech.
   D) the speaker must decide on the conclusion first so that the same device can be used in the introduction.

   Answer: A
   Diff: 2   Page Ref: 328
   Skill: Factual

29) In a speech introduction, it is important to:
   A) give few interesting details from the body of the speech.
   B) tell the audience you researched the information in the speech.
   C) indicate to the audience why the speaker is talking to them about this topic.
   D) find out from the audience whether anyone is familiar with the speech topic.

   Answer: C
   Diff: 2   Page Ref: 328
   Skill: Interpretive

30) In concluding speech, the text indicated that the speaker needs some kind of closure. This means:
   A) the speaker keeps on explaining until everyone understands.
   B) the speaker lets the listeners draw their own thoughts from his or her main points.
   C) the speaker says "That's it. Thank you very much."
   D) the speaker ends in a clear and distinct manner.

   Answer: D
   Diff: 2   Page Ref: 329–330
   Skill: Interpretive

31) The conclusion should fulfill all of the following functions EXCEPT:
   A) it should summarize the main points.
   B) it should achieve some find of closure.
   C) it should provide some final motivation
   D) it should allow the audience to make up its own mind

   Answer: D
   Diff: 2   Page Ref: 329–330
   Skill: Factual

TRUE/FALSE. Write 'T' if the statement is true and 'F' if the statement is false.

1) Your author advises you to word your thesis as a compound or complex sentence.

Answer: FALSE
Diff: 2   Page Ref: 308
Skill: Factual

2) Narratives are specific instances that are explained in varying degrees of detail.

Answer: TRUE
Diff: 2   Page Ref: 311
Skill: Factual

3) Narratives are the opinions of experts and the accounts of witnesses.

Answer: FALSE
Diff: 2   Page Ref: 311
Skill: Interpretive

4) If you wanted to demonstrate the muscles of the body, you might use a bodybuilder as a presentation aid.

Answer: TRUE
Diff: 1   Page Ref: 314
Skill: Interpretive

5) Low tech media materials are generally more effective with large or formal groups where you will do most of the talking and the audience most of the listening.

Answer: FALSE
Diff: 2   Page Ref: 316–319
Skill: Interpretive

6) Your author advises that you prepare your presentation aids to make sure that they add clarity to your speech, that they're appealing to the listeners, and that they are culturally sensitive.

Answer: TRUE
Diff: 2   Page Ref: 316–319
Skill: Factual

7) Using the American dollar sign to symbolize "wealth" would be logical with an audience of international visitors.

Answer: FALSE
Diff: 2   Page Ref: 316–319
Skill: Factual

8) A good guideline to follow in designing your slides is to give each item heading in your outline that has the same level a different typeface, size, and color throughout your presentation.

Answer: FALSE
Diff: 2   *Page Ref: 317*
Skill: Factual

9) Organization with a temporal pattern is difficult for an audience to follow.

Answer: FALSE
Diff: 1   *Page Ref: 324–325*
Skill: Factual

10) Organization helps you prepare a speech.

Answer: TRUE
Diff: 1   *Page Ref: 324–326*
Skill: Factual

11) The problem–solution pattern of organization is identical to the effect–cause pattern.

Answer: FALSE
Diff: 1   *Page Ref: 325–326*
Skill: Factual

12) In the motivated sequence organizational pattern, visualization intensifies the audiences' feelings or beliefs.

Answer: TRUE
Diff: 2   *Page Ref: 326*
Skill: Factual

13) The multiple definition pattern is often useful for explaining specific concepts.

Answer: TRUE
Diff: 1   *Page Ref: 328*
Skill: Factual

14) Your introduction serves only to gain attention.

Answer: FALSE
Diff: 1   *Page Ref: 328*
Skill: Factual

15) A clever and appropriate anecdote is often useful in holding attention.

Answer: TRUE
Diff: 2   *Page Ref: 328*
Skill: Factual

16) Little-known facts or statistics will lose an audience's attention.

Answer: FALSE
Diff: 1   *Page Ref: 328*
Skill: Factual

17) The thesis of a speech is the main idea the speaker wants to get across to the audience.

Answer: TRUE
Diff: 1   *Page Ref: 309*
Skill: Factual

18) The longer the conclusion, the better.

Answer: FALSE
Diff: 1   *Page Ref: 329–330*
Skill: Factual

19) Each main point in a speech needs to have supporting material.

Answer: TRUE
Diff: 1   *Page Ref: 308–310*
Skill: Factual

CHAPTER 17   Style and Delivery in Public Speaking

MULTIPLE CHOICE. Choose the one alternative that best completes the statement or answers the question.

1) Which of these is a thesis for a speech?

A) The mass media set the public agenda.

B) To inform my audience of two major functions of the mass media.

C) To inform and persuade.

D) To persuade my audience about the agenda setting function of the mass media.

Answer: A
Diff: 2   Page Ref: 335-337
Skill: Applied

2) Which guideline for constructing your outline is offered?

A) Outline the introduction, body, and conclusion as one unit.

B) Use two ideas for each symbol.

C) Phrase your ideas as questions or phrases.

D) Append a list of references.

Answer: D
Diff: 2   Page Ref: 335
Skill: Factual

3) Which is true about oral style in comparison with written style?

A) You speak as you write.

B) Spoken language has shorter, simpler, and more familiar words.

C) Spoken language has fewer pseudo–quantifying terms.

D) Spoken language has fewer "allness" terms.

Answer: B
Diff: 2   Page Ref: 342
Skill: Factual

4) Which is offered as a guideline to clarity in speaking?

A) Favor the more commonly used term over the rarely used term.

B) Favor the long word over the short word.

C) Use general terms and numbers.

D) Favor the unfamiliar word over the familiar word.

Answer: A
Diff: 2   Page Ref: 343
Skill: Factual

5) Many commonly use words are confused. Which of the following pairs of words is CONFUSED?

   A) Use "accept" to mean receive and "except" to mean with the exclusion of.

   B) Use "between" when referring to two items and "among" when referring to more than two items.

   C) Use "to infer" to mean to state indirectly and "to infer" to mean to draw a conclusion.

   D) Use "can" to refer to ability and "may" to refer to permission.

Answer: C
Diff: 2   *Page Ref: 343*
Skill: Factual

6) Which is FALSE about making your language vivid?

   A) Favor verbs that communicate possibility rather than activity.

   B) Use strong verbs.

   C) Use figures of speech.

   D) Make us see, hear, and feel what you're talking about through imagery.

Answer: A
Diff: 2   *Page Ref: 344*
Skill: Factual

7) "City Hall issued the following news release" best illustrates this figure of speech.

   A) alliteration

   B) metonymy

   C) antithesis

   D) rhetorical question

Answer: B
Diff: 2   *Page Ref: 344*
Skill: Applied

8) "It was the best of times, it was the worst of times" best illustrates this figure of speech.

   A) metaphor

   B) rhetorical question

   C) alleration

   D) antithesis

Answer: D
Diff: 2   *Page Ref: 344*
Skill: Applied

9) What does your author suggest you do to make your language appropriate?

A) Generally avoid ethnic expressions.

B) Use unfamiliar terms.

C) Use formal language

D) Use slang.

Answer: A
Diff: 2   Page Ref: 345
Skill: Factual

10) What does your author NOT suggest you use to create a personal style of speaking?

A) Learning about your listeners' personal lives.

B) Use personal pronouns.

C) Use questions.

D) Create immediacy.

Answer: A
Diff: 2   Page Ref: 346
Skill: Factual

11) How can we create immediacy?

A) Refer to differences between you and your audience.

B) Use terms that include you and your audience, such as "we" and "our."

C) Address the audience indirectly as "students" instead of "you."

D) Avoid personal examples.

Answer: A
Diff: 2   Page Ref: 346
Skill: Applied

12) Your author suggests that to empower your speaking, you should avoid tag questions. Which is a tag question?

A) I'm not very good at this.

B) I'll review the report now, okay?

C) Really, this was the greatest.

D) No problem.

Answer: B
Diff: 2   Page Ref: 348
Skill: Applied

13) Your author suggests that to empower your speaking, you should avoid self-critical statements because
   A) they make you sound unprepared and uncertain.
   B) they signal low social class and hence little power.
   C) they signal a lack of confidence and make public your inadequacies.
   D) they make your speeches all sound the same.

   Answer: C
   Diff: 2   *Page Ref: 348*
   Skill: Factual

14) Which is a bromide?
   A) In this day and age.
   B) Few and far between.
   C) In the pink.
   D) If I can't do it well, I won't do it at all.

   Answer: D
   Diff: 2   *Page Ref: 347*
   Skill: Factual

15) Which is a cliche?
   A) She's as pretty as a picture.
   B) Honesty is the best policy.
   C) The life of the party.
   D) I don't understand modern art, but I know what I like.

   Answer: C
   Diff: 2   *Page Ref: 347-348*
   Skill: Factual

16) To make your language forceful, your author advises you to do all of these EXCEPT
   A) eliminate weakness.
   B) use bromides and cliches.
   C) vary intensity as appropriate.
   D) cut out any unnecessary phrases that reduce the impact of your meaning.

   Answer: B
   Diff: 2   *Page Ref: 346-347*
   Skill: Factual

17) Which of the following is advised for phrasing sentences?

    A) Use long sentences.

    B) Use passive sentences.

    C) Use positive sentences.

    D) Avoid varying the types of sentences you use.

Answer: C
Diff: 2   *Page Ref: 347–348*
Skill: Factual

18) Which of these sentences is easier to comprehend and remember, according to your author?

    A) The committee did not accept the proposal.

    B) The committee rejected the proposal.

    C) The committee does not work well together.

    D) The committee has not been productive.

Answer: B
Diff: 3   *Page Ref: 349*
Skill: Interpretive

19) Active sentences are easier to understand. Which is an active sentence?

    A) The appeal was rejected by the court.

    B) The request was granted by the committee.

    C) The administration favored the proposal.

    D) The proposal was ignored by management.

Answer: C
Diff: 2   *Page Ref: 348*
Skill: Interpretive

20) What advice is given for rehearsing your speech?

    A) Rehearse the speech in parts.

    B) Time the speech only on your last rehearsal.

    C) Rehearse the speech no less than ten times.

    D) Rehearse the speech in front of a full-length mirror.

Answer: D
Diff: 2   *Page Ref: 349–351*
Skill: Factual

21) This method of speech delivery involves thorough preparation but no commitment to the exact wording to be used during the speech.

   A) impromptu

   B) manuscript

   C) extemporaneous

   D) memorized

Answer: C

Diff: 2   Page Ref: 352–353

Skill: Factual

22) Effective delivery includes all of these EXCEPT:

   A) effective delivery is natural.

   B) effective delivery reinforces the message.

   C) effective delivery is unvaried.

   D) effective delivery is conversational.

Answer: C

Diff: 2   Page Ref: 349–351

Skill: Factual

23) Which dimension of voice comes into play most when you emphasize a word in a sentence such as: Is THIS the proposal you want me to support?

   A) volume

   B) loudness

   C) rate

   D) pitch

Answer: D

Diff: 2   Page Ref: 358

Skill: Factual

24) The way you use space in communication is known as

   A) gesture.

   B) movement.

   C) proxemics.

   D) posture.

Answer: C

Diff: 2   Page Ref: 360

Skill: Factual

25) Jamieson and Campbell suggest that you can effectively influence the media in which way?

    A) Write letters to the editor of a newspaper.

    B) Call in to a television talk show.

    C) Write letters to the Federal Communication Commission.

    D) Use group pressure to bear on networks and newspapers.

    E) all of the above

Answer: E
Diff: 2   *Page Ref: 357*
Skill: Factual

26) Which statement best describes the term "oral style"?

    A) a quality of spoken language that clearly separates it from written language

    B) composing your thoughts after considerable reflection followed by editing

    C) oral language that requires thought for interpretation and understanding

    D) abstract terms, few qualifiers, complex and technical word usage

Answer: A
Diff: 2   *Page Ref: 342*
Skill: Interpretive

TRUE/FALSE. Write 'T' if the statement is true and 'F' if the statement is false.

1) Outlines should be neither extremely general nor extremely detailed.

Answer: FALSE
Diff: 1   *Page Ref: 335*
Skill: Factual

2) Generally, spoken language consists of shorter, simpler, and more familiar words than does written language.

Answer: TRUE
Diff: 1   *Page Ref: 342*
Skill: Interpretive

3) Written language has a greater number of self-reference terms than spoken language.

Answer: FALSE
Diff: 1   *Page Ref: 342*
Skill: Factual

4) For the most part, it is wise to use "written style" in your public speeches.

Answer: FALSE
Diff: 1   *Page Ref: 342*
Skill: Factual

5) Clarity in speaking style should be your primary goal.

Answer: TRUE
Diff: 1   Page Ref: 343
Skill: Factual

6) The negative side of idioms is that they give your speech a casual and informal style.

Answer: FALSE
Diff: 2   Page Ref: 344
Skill: Factual

7) Your author advises you to favor verbs that communicate passivity rather than activity.

Answer: FALSE
Diff: 1   Page Ref: 348
Skill: Interpretive

8) The slogan "fifty-four forty or fight" illustrates alliteration.

Answer: TRUE
Diff: 1   Page Ref: 344
Skill: Factual

9) Auditory imagery allows your listeners to feel the cool water running over their bodies and the punch of a fighter.

Answer: FALSE
Diff: 1   Page Ref: 344
Skill: Factual

10) Your author advises you to avoid unfamiliar terms and to avoid slang.

Answer: TRUE
Diff: 1   Page Ref: 343
Skill: Factual

11) Audiences favor speakers who speak in an impersonal rather than a personal style.

Answer: FALSE
Diff: 1   Page Ref: 346
Skill: Factual

12) Immediacy is a connectedness with your listeners.

Answer: TRUE
Diff: 1   Page Ref: 346
Skill: Interpretive

13) To create immediacy, you should use terms like "we" and "our."

Answer: TRUE
Diff: 1   Page Ref: 346
Skill: Applied

14) You should eliminate weak sentences and modifiers.

Answer: TRUE
Diff: 1   Page Ref: 346-349
Skill: Factual

15) You should delete any unnecessary phrases that reduce the impact of your meaning.

Answer: TRUE
Diff: 1   Page Ref: 347-349
Skill: Factual

16) Slang and vulgarity communicate a lack of respect for your audience.

Answer: TRUE
Diff: 1   Page Ref: 345
Skill: Interpretive

17) Hesitations make you sound prepared and certain.

Answer: FALSE
Diff: 1   Page Ref: 348
Skill: Factual

18) The phrase "black as coal" is a cliche.

Answer: TRUE
Diff: 1   Page Ref: 347-348
Skill: Applied

19) Short sentences are easier to comprehend and remember than long sentences.

Answer: TRUE
Diff: 1   Page Ref: 349
Skill: Interpretive

20) Rehearse your speech as often as seems necessary.

Answer: TRUE
Diff: 1   Page Ref: 351
Skill: Factual

21) When you speak extemporaneously, you speak without any specific preparation.

Answer: FALSE
Diff: 1   Page Ref: 353
Skill: Factual

22) In the manuscript method of speaking, you memorize your speech and "act it out."

Answer: FALSE
Diff: 1   Page Ref: 352
Skill: Factual

23) Effective delivery is varied.

Answer: TRUE
Diff: 1   Page Ref: 354
Skill: Factual

24) Effective delivery is conversational.

Answer: TRUE
Diff: 1   Page Ref: 354
Skill: Factual

25) The most important single aspect of bodily communication is proxemics.

Answer: FALSE
Diff: 1   Page Ref: 359-360
Skill: Factual

CHAPTER 18   The Informative Speech

MULTIPLE CHOICE. Choose the one alternative that best completes the statement or answers the question.

1) What advice is offered about limiting the amount of information to your audience in an informative speech?
   A) Expand the breadth of information you communicate.
   B) Limit the depth of information you communicate.
   C) It is better to present five items of information without amplification than to present two new items and explain these with examples, illustrations, and descriptions.
   D) Resist the temptation to overload your listeners with information.

   Answer: D
   Diff: 2   *Page Ref: 363*
   Skill: Factual

2) Stated in the form of suggestions for informative speaking, which is true about the most frequently noted ways for stressing relevance to your audience?
   A) Use examples that make content relevant.
   B) Relate current events to the content of your talk.
   C) Explain how the content is related to career goals of your listeners.
   D) All of the above
   E) None of the above

   Answer: D
   Diff: 2   *Page Ref: 363–364*
   Skill: Factual

3) This strategy for describing might describe the layout of Winnipeg by starting from the north and working down to the south.
   A) using presentational aids
   B) selecting an appropriate organizational pattern
   C) using a variety of descriptive categories
   D) considering who, what, where, when, and why

   Answer: B
   Diff: 2   *Page Ref: 367*
   Skill: Interpretive

4) In defining the word "communication", you note that it comes from the Latin "communis", meaning "common." This is definition by

   A) authority.

   B) negation.

   C) etymology.

   D) direct symbolization.

Answer: C
Diff: 2   *Page Ref: 368–369*
Skill: Applied

5) In defining a "wife" as "not a cook, not a cleaning person, not a seamstress", you define by

   A) authority.

   B) negation.

   C) etymology.

   D) direct symbolization.

Answer: B
Diff: 2   *Page Ref: 368–369*
Skill: Applied

6) Which statement is true?

   A) The knowledge gap refers to the difference in knowledge between one group and another.

   B) Research has focused on the influence of the media in narrowing the knowledge gap.

   C) Information is inexpensive and everyone has easy access to it.

   D) Japanese is the language that dominates the Internet.

Answer: A
Diff: 2   *Page Ref: 366*
Skill: Factual

TRUE/FALSE. Write 'T' if the statement is true and 'F' if the statement is false.

1) There is no limit to the amount of information that a listener can take in at one time.

Answer: FALSE
Diff: 1   *Page Ref: 363*
Skill: Factual

2) Generally, beginning speakers err on the side of being too complex.

Answer: TRUE
Diff: 1   *Page Ref: 363*
Skill: Interpretive

3) Listeners will remember your information best when they see it as relevant and useful to their own needs or goals.

Answer: TRUE
Diff: 1   *Page Ref: 363–364*
Skill: Interpretive

4) One study found that the greater the relevance of the lecture, the less the students were motivated to study.

Answer: FALSE
Diff: 2   *Page Ref: 380363–364*
Skill: Factual

5) Listeners will learn information more easily and retain it longer when you relate it to what they already know.

Answer: TRUE
Diff: 1   *Page Ref: 364–365*
Skill: Factual

6) Through phonetic change, the Anglo-Saxon "wifman" became "woman."

Answer: TRUE
Diff: 1   *Page Ref: 369*
Skill: Factual

7) Your author advises you to start with what is new to your audience and work up to what they know.

Answer: FALSE
Diff: 2   *Page Ref: 364–365*
Skill: Interpretive

8) It is often helpful when demonstrating to present each step in detail and then give a broad general picture.

Answer: FALSE
Diff: 2   *Page Ref: 371*
Skill: Factual

9) Visual aids are of no help in showing the steps of a process in a sequence.

Answer: FALSE
Diff: 1   *Page Ref: 367*
Skill: Factual

10) False Memory Syndrome is a theory for reducing uncertainty.

Answer: FALSE
Diff: 1   *Page Ref: 374–377*
Skill: Factual

11) The knowledge gap refers to the difference between those who have a great deal of knowledge and those who have significantly less.

Answer: TRUE
Diff: 1   *Page Ref: 366*
Skill: Factual

12) Only 15% of the children in families with incomes under $20,000 have a computer in the home.

Answer: TRUE
Diff: 1   *Page Ref: 366*
Skill: Interpretive

13) Seventy-four percent of the children in families with incomes over $75,000 have a computer in the home.

Answer: TRUE
Diff: 1   *Page Ref: 366*
Skill: Factual

14) English dominates the Internet.

Answer: TRUE
Diff: 1   *Page Ref: 366*
Skill: Factual

15) While India is having great difficulty developing software that will sell throughout the world, Japan is enjoying an enormously successful software industry.

Answer: FALSE
Diff: 2   *Page Ref: 366*
Skill: Factual

CHAPTER 19   The Persuasive Speech

MULTIPLE CHOICE. Choose the one alternative that best completes the statement or answers the question.

1) Which is a question of policy?
   A) Is bullfighting inhumane?
   B) Does television violence lead to violent behavior in teens?
   C) What should our position be on affirmative action?
   D) Are IQ tests biased?

   Answer: C
   Diff: 2   Page Ref: 380–383
   Skill: Interpretive

2) Which is a question of value?
   A) Is doctor-assisted suicide humane?
   B) Is Iraq hiding chemical weapons?
   C) Do lesbians constitute less than 10% of all women in the military?
   D) What should our drug policy be?

   Answer: A
   Diff: 2   Page Ref: 380–383
   Skill: Interpretive

3) Which is a question of fact?
   A) What should the college's sexual harassment policy be?
   B) Do college students today drink more beer than college students did 20 years ago?
   C) What should be done with drunken drivers?
   D) Is the death penalty morally justifiable?

   Answer: B
   Diff: 2   Page Ref: 380–383
   Skill: Interpretive

4) In this unethical persuasive technique, the speaker gives an idea, a group of people, or a political philosophy a bad name.
   A) bandwagon
   B) testimonial
   C) name-calling
   D) agenda-setting

   Answer: C
   Diff: 2   Page Ref: 382–383
   Skill: Factual

5) In this unethical persuasive technique, the speaker selects only the evidence and arguments that support the case and might even falsify evidence and distort the facts to better fit the case.

A) transfer

B) card-stocking

C) transfer

D) attack

Answer: B
Diff: 2   Page Ref: 382-383
Skill: Factual

6) In this unethical persuasive technique, the speaker argues that XYZ is the issue and that all other issues are unimportant and insignificant.

A) attack

B) bandwagon

C) plain folks

D) agenda-setting

Answer: D
Diff: 2   Page Ref: 382-383
Skill: Factual

7) Which is true of the law of selective exposure?
A) Listeners actively seek out information that contradicts their existing opinions, beliefs, attitudes, values, and behaviors.
B) Listeners actively avoid information that supports their opinions, beliefs, values, decisions, and behaviors.
C) Listeners actively seek out information that supports their opinions, beliefs, values, decisions, and behaviors.

Answer: C
Diff: 2   Page Ref: 383-384
Skill: Factual

8) What is true about culture and influence?

A) Members of different cultures respond the same to persuasive attempts.

B) A religious leader's credibility is assessed as believable equally across cultures.
C) Asian audiences favor hearing the general principle first and the evidence, examples, and argument second.
D) Schools in the United States teach students to demand logical and reliable evidence before believing something.
E) Low context cultures generally expect an explicit and prefer a very explicit statement of what the speaker wants the audience to do.

Answer: D
Diff: 3   Page Ref: 384-385
Skill: Factual

9) Which is FALSE of persuasion?
   A) Persuasion is greatest when the audience participates actively in your presentation.
   B) Listeners who paraphrase or summarize are more persuaded than those who receive the message passively.
   C) If you're addressing an inoculated audience, you should consider the fact that your listeners have a ready arsenal of counter-arguments to fight your persuasive message.
   D) With a well-inoculated audience, you should try to reverse their beliefs totally.

   Answer: D
   Diff: 3   *Page Ref: 385-386*
   Skill: Factual

10) Which is true about the magnitude of change?
    A) If you try to convince your audience to change their attitudes radically or to engage in behaviors to which they are initially opposed, your attempts may backfire.
    B) The greater and more important the change you want to produce in your audience, the easier your task will be.
    C) People change suddenly, as a rule, in large degrees over a long period of time.
    D) Persuasion is most effective when it strives for large changes and works over a short period of time.
    E) You are less easily persuaded and demand more evidence on relatively minor issues.

    Answer: A
    Diff: 3   *Page Ref: 386-387*
    Skill: Factual

11) You first request something small, something that your audience will easily comply with. Once you achieve this, you then make your large request. This persuasive technique is called
    A) the door-in-the-face technique.
    B) the knife-in-the-back technique.
    C) the foot-in-the-door technique.
    D) the foot-in-the-mouth technique.

    Answer: C
    Diff: 2   *Page Ref: 386-387*
    Skill: Factual

12) In this persuasive strategy, you make a large request that you know will be refused. Later, you make a moderate request, the one you really want your listeners to comply with.
    A) the foot-in-the-door technique
    B) the knife-in-the-back technique
    C) the foot-in-the-mouth technique
    D) the door-in-the-face technique

    Answer: D
    Diff: 2   *Page Ref: 387*
    Skill: Interpretive

13) All of the following statements about reducing dissonance are true EXCEPT:

A) Generally, direct your propositions at increasing your audience's sense of consistency.

B) If the audience is experiencing dissonance, try to connect your thesis or propositions to its reduction.

C) When dissonance occurs, you will try to do something to increase it.

D) If you can show your audience how they can easily change their behavior to be consistent with their attitudes, you will have a favorably disposed audience.

Answer: D
Diff: 2   Page Ref: 387
Skill: Interpretive

14) In this test of evidence and argument, you gather evidence and arguments from numerous and diverse sources in drawing a conclusion or supporting a thesis.

A) recency

B) corroboration

C) fairness

D) bias

Answer: D
Diff: 2   Page Ref: 387–388
Skill: Interpretive

15) This aspect of public communication consists basically of arguments with evidence and a conclusion.

A) mythos

B) pathos

C) logos

D) ethos

Answer: B
Diff: 2   Page Ref: 388
Skill: Interpretive

16) When speakers appeal to their audience to help others, feed the hungry, and cure the sick, they appeal primarily to this motive.

A) fear

B) power, control, and influence

C) achievement

D) altruism

E) status

Answer: D
Diff: 2   Page Ref: 388
Skill: Factual

17) When speakers appeal to their audience to become what they feel they are fit for, to be all that they can be, or to be the best that they can be, they appeal primarily to this motive.

A) achievement

B) self-actualization

C) affiliation

D) conformity

E) approval

Answer: B

Diff: 2   Page Ref: 389–390

Skill: Interpretive

18) This quality of credibility refers to the knowledge and expertise the audience thinks the speaker has.

A) character

B) charisma

C) competence

D) logos

Answer: C

Diff: 2   Page Ref: 389–390

Skill: Interpretive

19) This quality credibility refers to the intentions and concerns of the speaker for the audience.

A) character

B) charisma

C) logos

D) competence

Answer: A

Diff: 2   Page Ref: 391–392

Skill: Factual

20) The halo effect and reverse halo effect is associated with which quality of credibility?

A) charisma

B) competence

C) character

D) pathos

Answer: B

Diff: 2   Page Ref: 391–392

Skill: Factual

21) There are several strategies offered for strengthening or changing your listeners' attitudes, beliefs, and values. Which is NOT one of them?

A) Carefully estimate the current state of your listeners' attitudes, beliefs, and values.

B) Seek big changes in your listeners' attitudes and beliefs.

C) Demonstrate your credibility to your listeners.

D) Give your listeners good reasons for believing what you want them to believe.

Answer: B
Diff: 3   Page Ref: 392
Skill: Factual

22) There are several strategies offered for stimulating listeners to action. Which is NOT one of them?

A) Set reasonable goals for what you want your audience to do.

B) Ask your audience to do what you have not done yourself.

C) Stress the specific advantages of some action to your specific audience.

D) As a general rule, never ask your audience to do what you have not done yourself.

Answer: B
Diff: 3   Page Ref: 395-396
Skill: Interpretive

23) What does research support from scores on the Mach scale?

A) Low Machs are more resistant to persuasion.

B) High Machs are more easily susceptible to social influence.

C) Low Machs are more logical while high Machs are more empathic.

D) Low Machs are more assertive and controlling while high Machs are more interpersonally oriented.

Answer: C
Diff: 3   Page Ref: 398-399
Skill: Interpretive

24) Which of these statements is true?

A) Chinese students attending a traditional Chinese (Confucian) school rated higher in machiavellianism than similar Chinese students attending a Western-style school.

B) Self-monitors change the behaviors of theory to get what why want while Machiavellians change their own behaviors as a way of pleasing and manipulating others.

C) High Mach women are preferred as dating partners by both high and low Mach men.

D) High Machs earn higher grades in communication courses that involve face-to-face interaction.

E) Low Machs are generally more effective in all aspects of communication studied.

Answer: D
Diff: 3   Page Ref: 397-398
Skill: Factual

25) The statement "the greater and more important the change you want to produce in your audience, the more difficult your task will be," is a description of which principle of persuasion?

A) the magnitude of change principle

B) foot-in-the-door technique

C) the audience participation principle

D) the inoculation principle

Answer: A

Diff: 2   Page Ref: 397–398

Skill: Factual

26) Which statement best describes the inoculation principle of persuasion?

A) Persuasion is greatest when the audience participates actively in your presentation.

B) Audiences are more easily persuaded and demand less evidence on relatively minor issues.

C) The first request you make must be something small that your audience will easily comply with.

D) With no previous challenge to your beliefs and attitudes, you are more susceptible to persuasion.

Answer: D

Diff: 2   Page Ref: 386–387

Skill: Interpretive

27) When you first make a large request that you know will be refused and later you make a more moderate request, this persuasive technique is called

A) door-in-the-face technique.

B) face-in-the-door technique.

C) foot-in-the-door technique.

D) foot-in-the-face technique.

Answer: A

Diff: 2   Page Ref: 387

Skill: Factual

28) When a speaker presents evidence and arguments gathered from numerous and diverse sources, the speaker is said to be using

A) fairness.

B) recency.

C) corroboration.

D) logic.

Answer: C

Diff: 1   Page Ref: 388

Skill: Factual

29) Which of the following statements is NOT true about motives in persuasion?

A) Not all motives are equal in intensity.

B) Motives are static.

C) Satisfied needs do not motivate.

D) Motives differ from one time to another and from one person to another.

Answer: B
Diff: 1   Page Ref: 389–390
Skill: Factual

30) When people are motivated to do what they consider the right thing, they illustrate which motivational appeal?

A) power, control, and influence

B) love and affiliation

C) self–actualization

D) altruism

Answer: D
Diff: 2   Page Ref: 389–390
Skill: Factual

31) How believable you are as a speaker describes your

A) status.

B) credibility.

C) altruism.

D) motives.

Answer: B
Diff: 1   Page Ref: 391
Skill: Factual

32) Which of the following qualities is NOT a quality with which we identify the speaker's credibility?

A) competence

B) sincerity

C) character

D) charisma

Answer: B
Diff: 1   Page Ref: 392–393
Skill: Factual

TRUE/FALSE. Write 'T' if the statement is true and 'F' if the statement is false.

1) Questions of policy concern what is or is not true.

Answer: FALSE
Diff: 1   Page Ref: 382
Skill: Factual

2) Questions of fact concern what a person considers good or bad, moral or immoral, just or unjust.

Answer: FALSE
Diff: 1   Page Ref: 380
Skill: Factual

3) Questions of value concern what should be done and what practice should be followed.

Answer: FALSE
Diff: 1   Page Ref: 380
Skill: Factual

4) A single speech may involve questions of fact, value, and policy.

Answer: TRUE
Diff: 1   Page Ref: 380–382
Skill: Factual

5) A "glittering generality" occurs when a speaker tries to make you accept some idea by associating it with things you value highly.

Answer: TRUE
Diff: 2   Page Ref: 382–383
Skill: Factual

6) In the "plain folks" method, the speaker persuades the audience to accept or reject an idea because "everybody's doing it" or because the "right" people are doing it.

Answer: FALSE
Diff: 2   Page Ref: 382–383
Skill: Applied

7) "Agenda-setting" involves accusing another person, usually an opponent, of some serious wrongdoing so that the issue under discussion never gets examined.

Answer: FALSE
Diff: 2   Page Ref: 382–383
Skill: Factual

8) Listeners actively avoid information that contradicts their existing opinions, beliefs, attitudes, values, and behaviors.

Answer: TRUE
Diff: 1   Page Ref: 383–384
Skill: Factual

9) Asian audiences favor a deductive pattern of reasoning.

Answer: FALSE
Diff: 1   Page Ref: 384
Skill: Factual

10) High context cultures (Japanese, Chinese, and Arabic, for example) prefer an explicit statement of the speaker's position and of what he or she wants the audience to do.

Answer: FALSE
Diff: 2   Page Ref: 384
Skill: Factual

11) Persuasion is greatest when the audience participates actively in your presentation.

Answer: TRUE
Diff: 1   Page Ref: 384–385
Skill: Factual

12) Demagogues and propagandists never have their audiences chant slogans and repeat catch phrases.

Answer: FALSE
Diff: 1   Page Ref: 385–386
Skill: Factual

13) When addressing an inoculated audience, you have an audience with no counter-arguments to resist your persuasion.

Answer: FALSE
Diff: 1   Page Ref: 385–386
Skill: Factual

14) By presenting counter-arguments and then refuting them, you will enable your listeners to immunize themselves against future attacks on these values and beliefs.

Answer: TRUE
Diff: 2   Page Ref: 385–386
Skill: Factual

15) Persuasion is most effective when it strives for small changes and works over a considerable time period.

Answer: TRUE
Diff: 1   Page Ref: 386–387
Skill: Factual

16) In the foot-in-the-door technique, you first make a large request and later a more modest request.

Answer: FALSE
Diff: 1   Page Ref: 387
Skill: Factual

17) Dissonance may occur when attitudes contradict behavior.

Answer: TRUE
Diff: 1   Page Ref: 387–388
Skill: Factual

18) Recency, corroboration, and fairness are the three general tests of evidence and argument.

Answer: TRUE
Diff: 1   Page Ref: 388
Skill: Interpretive

19) When your audience appeals are to pathos, you direct your energies to your audience's needs and desires.

Answer: TRUE
Diff: 1   Page Ref: 389–390
Skill: Factual

20) In Maslow's system of needs, certain needs have to be satisfied before other needs can motivate behavior.

Answer: TRUE
Diff: 1   Page Ref: 389–390
Skill: Factual

21) An inspirational speech with the theme of "you are the greatest" never appeals to our need for self-esteem and approval.

Answer: FALSE
Diff: 1   Page Ref: 389
Skill: Applied

22) Credibility is something a speaker has or does not have in an objective sense.

Answer: FALSE
Diff: 2   Page Ref: 391–392
Skill: Factual

23) Competence is usually limited to one specific field.

Answer: TRUE
Diff: 1   Page Ref: 392
Skill: Factual

24) Charisma refers to the personality and dynamism of the speaker.

Answer: TRUE
Diff: 1   Page Ref: 392
Skill: Factual

25) The halo effect occurs when listeners generalize their perception of competence to all areas.

Answer: TRUE
Diff: 1   Page Ref: 392
Skill: Factual

26) The public speaking audience expects the speaker to fool them.

Answer: FALSE
Diff: 1   Page Ref: 393
Skill: Factual

27) As a general rule, ask your audience to do what you have not done yourself.

Answer: FALSE
Diff: 1   Page Ref: 395–396
Skill: Interpretive

28) The term "Machiavellian" refers to the methods one person uses to help another fulfil himself or herself.

Answer: FALSE
Diff: 1   Page Ref: 397–398
Skill: Factual

29) High Machs are more easily susceptible to social influence than low Machs.

Answer: FALSE
Diff: 2   Page Ref: 397–398
Skill: Factual

30) Low Machs are more resistant to persuasion than high Machs.

Answer: FALSE
Diff: 2   Page Ref: 397–398
Skill: Factual

31) High Machs are more empathic while low Machs are more logical.

Answer: FALSE
Diff: 2   Page Ref: 397–398
Skill: Factual

32) Low Machs are more assertive and controlling than high Machs.

Answer: FALSE
Diff: 2   Page Ref: 397–398
Skill: Factual

33) High Machs are most effective at persuading others when the situation allows them to improvise.

Answer: TRUE
Diff: 2   Page Ref: 397–398
Skill: Factual

34) High Mach women are preferred as dating partners by both high and low Mach men.

Answer: FALSE
Diff: 2   Page Ref: 397–398
Skill: Factual

35) While self-monitors change their own behavior to get what they want from others, Machiavellians try to change the behavior of others to get what they want.

Answer: TRUE
Diff: 2   Page Ref: 397–398
Skill: Factual

36) The selective exposure principle holds that a listener will expose him/herself to high credibility sources more often than to low credibility sources.

Answer: FALSE
Diff: 2   Page Ref: 383–384
Skill: Factual

37) Generally, it is easier to persuade an uninoculated audience than an inoculated audience.

Answer: TRUE
Diff: 1   Page Ref: 385–386
Skill: Factual

38) Generally, we perceive as credible, people we like rather than people we do not like.

Answer: TRUE
Diff: 1   *Page Ref: 391–393*
Skill: Factual

39) Although competence is logically subject-specific, many people do not make distinctions between areas of competence and areas of incompetence when evaluating the speaker's credibility.

Answer: TRUE
Diff: 2   *Page Ref: 392*
Skill: Interpretive

40) Generally, it has been shown that the shy, introverted person will be perceived to have higher credibility than the aggressive, extroverted person.

Answer: FALSE
Diff: 2   *Page Ref: 391–393*
Skill: Factual

41) Listeners actively seek out information that supports their opinions, beliefs, values, decisions, and behaviors.

Answer: TRUE
Diff: 1   *Page Ref: 383–384*
Skill: Factual

42) According to Maslow's "hierarchy of needs," satisfied needs are highly motivating.

Answer: FALSE
Diff: 1   *Page Ref: 389–390*
Skill: Factual

43) Basically, our motives are fairly consistent over time and rarely change very much.

Answer: FALSE
Diff: 1   *Page Ref: 389–390*
Skill: Factual